FULLY BOOKED

The Hair Stylist's Guide to Building a Client Attraction System That Works

Marquetta Breslin

RMNC Publishing

RMNC Publishing

P.O. Box 2250
Summerville, SC 29484

Printed in the United States of America

First published in 2015 by RMNC Publishing, a member of Breslin Products, LLC.

Book Layout © 2015 Capstone Design Group LLC

Fully Booked / Marquetta Breslin – 1st Edition

ISBN 978-1-935020-26-4

Dedicated to my husband and business partner Ricky Breslin

CONTENTS

What Most Stylists Will Never Know About Getting Clients I

Why Most Stylists Do It Wrong! II

Attraction Is Not a Choice 1

Client Attraction Law #1: If You Chase Things, They Will Run Away! 3

Client Attraction from the Inside Out 4

You Were "Brainwashed" to Play Small 5

How to Become Instantly Attractive to the World 7

The Real You Is a Leader 8

You, the Trusted Advisor 11

The Golden Rule Works! 12

You're Not a Lawyer or a Doctor? You "Just" Style Hair? Thank God! 14

Who Buys You First? 15

The Recipe for Transforming Yourself into a Trusted Advisor 16

How Do You Attract More Clients by Talking Less about You? 16

Clients Don't Care about You 17

Clients Don't Care about You OR What You Do – They Only Care about
What They GET Because of What You Do! 18

The Needy Service Provider 20

The Biggest and Most Damaging Type of Need..22

You Will <u>Never</u> Reach Your Full Potential for Success In The Hair Industry
If You Care What Other People Think of You 23

Client Attraction Law #2: People are Extremely Attracted to People Who Don't Care
What Others Think about Them!..24

How to Banish Need Forever and Become More Attractive to Prospective Clients 25

Dear Stylist, So Why Should We Hire You and Not Someone Else?.................. 27

The Power of Clarity 28

Why This Is Work worth Doing...29

Why Seeing These Answers Can Be So Difficult..30

Does This Really Matter in the Real World? 31

What Happens to the Value of Something When It Is One of a Kind?...............32

As Demand for Something Exceeds Supply of That Something, Prices Go Up! 33

The 3-Step Process to Becoming a One-of-a-Kind Stylist 34

Step 1: Who Are We Talking About?..34

Step 2: What Pain Do You Relieve?...35

Step 3: Thinking about *Your* Journey..36

What to Do While You're Figuring Out All of This..37

The Power of the Platform! 39

Avoiding a Sure Path to Insanity 40

The Harsh Reality: You Don't Control Whether a Client Chooses to Sit in Your
Chair or Not...42

Put On Your Platform Shoes! 43

#1: They Must Know You Exist
#2: They Must Know You Are Skilled
#3: They Must Trust You...43

The Platform Is All about <u>Demonstration</u> 44

The Platform vs. "Advertising" 45

How to Create Your Client Attraction Platform Blueprint in Six Minutes (or Less!)......47

STEP 1: Double Check Your Target (Your Second Chance!) 48

STEP 2: Stepping into Their Shoes 50

STEP 3: Your BIG IDEAS...52

What Are These Big Ideas For?.. 55

STEP 4: Name, Format, and Frequency.. 55

How Is My Subscriber Better Off after Reading/Listening to This Than They
Were Before?... 58

Format and Frequency 59

What Does This Look Like in the Real World? 61

What's It Look Like and How Often Does It Appear?.................................. 61

Wrapping Your Platform in a Package That Sells! 62

What Do We Call It? 63

<u>Looking Great in Richmond</u>: Everything You Need to Know About
Living Beautiful!.. 64

Transforming Trust into Paying Clients **65**

Building an Open Door... 66

How to Craft an Invitation That Starts Things Off Right! 72

How to Become the Most Interesting Stylist in the World............................ **74**

What Do You Do When They Actually Show Up? 75

How to Control Any Conversation and Make Yourself Look Awesome!....................... 77

All Questions Are <u>Not</u> Created Equal 78

Can You Describe to Me What Your Picture of "Success" from Our Work
Together Looks Like? 80

Your Goal is <u>Not</u> to Sell! 81

Rewriting Your Money Programs and Charging Premium Fees........................ **83**

The Energy of Money 84

Energy and Client Attraction 84

How to Reset Your Relationship with Money... 85

You Have Systematically Been Taught That You Are Small and Weak and
Hardly Worthy of Much, Let Alone True Success...................................... 86

Make Today the Day You Begin the Journey towards Sending out A Clear Signal
about What You Want and How You Feel about Yourself............................. 88

How to Fill Your Being with the Energy That Is Attractive to EVERYTHING 89

What Is <u>Your</u> Station Broadcasting? 91

Stop Charging Money for Haircuts 92

How Much Could One Piece of Paper be Worth? 93

Stop Charging for What You Do! Start Charging for What They Get Because
of What You Do! 94

Why Getting Money Seems So Hard 95

Dealing with the Turbulence 98

How I Became a One-of-a-Kind Stylist and How You Can Too! 99

Packing Yourself Up in a Box **101**

The Power of Product 102

But I'm a Stylist! I Do Hair! I Can't Make Products! 103

The Good News 104

The Reason I Learned How to Make Lace Wigs 104

Multimedia, Multiple Levels of Value 106

But if I Solve These Problems for My Clients, Why Would They Come to See Me? 107

How to Put Your Products to Work for You, Even If You Never Sell One! 108

My Million Dollar Secret **111**

A New Way of Thinking About Anything Related to Business 112

Here's the Opposite of What We're Going to Do 113

"Million Dollar Secret Rule" #1: If the Marketing or Advertising Costs Money and
You Can't Prove It Worked, Do Something Else! 114

This is Not Only a More Effective Way of Marketing! It's a Completely Different
Way of Thinking! 120

The Missing Ingredients **122**

With Responsibility Comes an Enormous Amount of Power 123

The 7-Day Challenge 125

No One Will Respect Your Time until YOU Do 127

How to Eradicate Need in 3 Seconds 129

GRATITUDE 129

How to Stand in Your Power Even When Everything Goes to $*#@! 131

Looking Forward 134

You Are Pushing a Snowball up the Hill 135

About the Author 138

INTRODUCTION

WHAT MOST STYLISTS WILL NEVER KNOW ABOUT GETTING CLIENTS

Before we get started, I have a promise to make to you. At first, this promise might sound unbelievable. And frankly, you might even wonder if I've "lost my marbles." But stick with me because by the end of this short book, my promise to you is that you will never again look at the task of "getting clients" the same way. You will be forever changed.

With the material you are holding right now in your hands, you will have the tools to completely transform your approach to attracting a steady stream of clients who treat you like the expert you are.

Inside this book are the secrets that can make you magnetic to clients. If you've never experienced that, you are in for a treat! Now I call these "secrets" not because they are mystical or magical. I call them secrets because so few stylists know about them but soon you will. And with that knowledge put into practice, you will see your world transform right in front of your eyes.

Why Most Stylists Do It Wrong!

I have to warn you: the first thing I'm going to ask you to do in our journey together is not easy. But, you really must do this if you want to start attracting the best clients. What you have to do is this: forget everything you've been told about how to get clients. Really.

Like I said, it's no small order. The reason it's hard is because we've all been trained for years about what it means to go out and get clients in the hair industry. And sadly, what we've been taught is just flat out wrong.

For example, what if I told you that the best way to make sure you end up with more great clients is to stop trying to "get" clients? Sounds nuts, right? It's not. In fact, this is one of the secrets that most stylists will never discover about how attracting clients actually works.

Worse than that, you can think of everything you've seen about how to attract clients – everything you've watched OTHER stylists do – as a type of "brainwashing." We've all seen it so much that it's hard to even believe there might be another way. Not only is there another way, but there's also a better way. It's a way that will put you in control and will give you the tools and systems to attract clients on YOUR terms.

The problem, however, is that this "brainwashing" affects our eyes. It keeps us from seeing opportunity, even though it is everywhere.

In the coming pages I'm going to be extremely blunt. I'm going to be blunt about how the world really works when it comes to being an expert and getting clients in the hair industry.

Listen up! Life is way too short to play small, so if you're not the type of person who is ready to think big – if you're not willing to go out there as the best version of who you are meant to be – then this probably isn't for you. You're just not ready. It doesn't mean you won't be ready sometime. It just means that right now isn't that time. That's fine. Put down this book and come back to it later.

If you're still reading, then hold onto your hat because we're about to take a journey that's going to transform your future in the hair industry forever....

1

ATTRACTION IS NOT A CHOICE

Attraction is one of the most powerful forces in the universe. So, when you're looking to build your success in the hair industry, this is the force that will help you do it. But, to use it, you have to understand it. And, more specifically, you have to be able to connect that understanding to real world action steps you actually take to make it happen for you.

In the coming pages that's exactly what we're going to do. First, we'll take a journey through how it works. Then we'll break it down so you can see how to make it work for you.

It's just the natural order of things that causes certain things to be attracted to certain other things. Of course, there's romantic attraction and that's part of it. Funny enough, there's a lot we can learn about "romantic attraction" that we can use in our work as stylists. The reason is simple. When it comes to attraction, we're dealing with universal principles. We're dealing with "laws" that are simply true all of the time. Don't trust me on this, though. Try it for yourself. The only validation you need is experience. You'll see.

....

Attraction is one of the most powerful forces in the universe.

....

My hunch is that you're going to be pretty amazed when you see how this works in the real world. But before we dig deep into what attraction IS, let me give you a really clear example of what attraction is NOT.

Imagine you're in the middle of the African desert. You're just sitting there, watching. You're invisible to all of the wildlife that is in the area, so they are just going about their business. It's not long before a lion comes out of the brush and sets its sights on an antelope in the distance. Little does the antelope know, it's about to become lunch.

The lion paces around waiting to make its move. Eventually, it sees an opportunity, and it bolts straight toward the antelope. The minute the antelope feels it is being pursued, a powerful force from deep inside propels it in the direction AWAY from the lion.

All of this is common sense, right? Wouldn't you run away from a lion if it was chasing you? That brings us to Client Attraction Law #1....

Client Attraction Law #1:
If You Chase Things, They Will Run Away!

This makes perfect sense if you think about it. Wouldn't you run away if someone was chasing you? Of course you would! So would I.

But this is exactly what most stylists do. They might not think they are chasing clients but they are. After all, how do you get them if you don't actually try to get them? The answer is you *attract* them.

You don't go to them. They come to you! You'll never hear this talked about in cosmetology school. They can't teach it because they don't even know it exists! And they certainly don't know how to do it. If you've ever heard that you should "start at the bottom and work your way up," that's a clue you're talking to someone who has no idea there's a much better, more fun, and more profitable way to go about creating success as a stylist.

Think about all of the things that stylists do to "get" clients. They discount their services. They never stop talking about "what they can do" for their clients. While those stylists might think they are actually contributing to their future success, I look at that and know they are doing the exact opposite. If you want clients who treat you like garbage and haggle over what you charge, what I just mentioned is exactly how you get them.

But, that's not the type of client I'm looking for. I want the client who chooses me over and above all of their other choices. I want the client who has the resources to invest in getting the best. I want the client who treats me like THE expert. I want the client who trusts my advice and the vision I have for her hair.

If that's the type of client you want, then you're in the right place. But understand this universal law: that client just doesn't show up by chance. You have to make it happen. You have to engineer what you do and how you do it so it can happen over and over again.

At this point in your journey, you might not think this is possible but it is. I know because I've lived it. I help stylists all over the world live it too.

The journey begins with a total transformation inside of you. Don't worry. I'm going to walk you through the entire thing. But first, I'm going to ask you to make a commitment to yourself. It's a commitment that will not only make you a better and more effective stylist, but it will also make you a better version of yourself.

Client Attraction from the Inside Out

So, here's how this is going to work. We're going to start at the beginning of this journey and work together towards the end. If you're a stylist looking to attract high quality clients, then it's important that you learn exactly where to begin this journey.

Most stylists have no idea, but I'm going to share it with you because it makes all the difference. And if you get this part right, the rest is pretty easy. So, go over to the nearest mirror and take a look. There's the beginning of your journey to becoming a master of client attraction. It's you. The source of all of your future clients is staring right back at you in the mirror.

Here's what I mean.

You have no idea just how powerful you are. And until you "realize" it and then figure out how to get that power out into the world, you're just going to stay right where you're at. Most people have zero chance to live a tomorrow that's too different than what they experience today. But, that's not you… not when you have what it takes to pick up a book like this.

You Were "Brainwashed" to Play Small

So here's the problem. You've spent years being tricked into believing that you can't have everything in your life that you want. I'm serious when I say this. You spent years being told to behave, to stand in line, to listen to the teacher, to get the right answer, to not stick out, to pretty much just blend in with the masses.

That might be a recipe for success in school, mind you, but that's not how it works in the real world. And certainly not when you're looking to achieve a level of success that most average folks wouldn't even think is possible.

So, if you're going to actually live your life as the success you are meant to be, then you have to clear out this programming and put something else in its place.

In school, we were taught that there is a right answer to everything. "What color is the sky?" The poor kid who was outside the night before and saw the sunset with all of its pink and purple coloring would get the question WRONG when he raised his hand and said, "pink and purple." "Oh, no. That's not right," said the teacher. "The color of the sky is blue."

And over and over we did this for years and years. I'm sure the teachers were not meaning you any harm, but practicing a habit like this does actually do something to your brain. What it does is this: it dampens your ability to direct your own life based on what YOU think and feel are the right things for you. What that means is that you end up looking around for someone to approve of what you are doing, or you look to someone else to tell you what to do.

....

You spent years being told to behave, to stand in line, to listen to the teacher, to get the right answer, to not stick out, to pretty much just blend in with the masses.

....

From my perspective, this is a miserable way to go through life. It's miserable because without breaking free of all of this programming, you will never be able to fully be the person you are meant to be.

It's not your fault, except now that you know it is your responsibility. Do you change that or do you just continue with the brainwashing?

If you're still reading, then let's do something about this so you can go out there and make an impact in the lives of your clients. Make a commitment to yourself that THIS is the day you stop accepting less than you KNOW you should have in your life.

Make this the day you STOP looking to others for direction....

Make this the day you DISCOVER the power that comes with not caring what others think of you....

Make THIS the day you say goodbye to the "small" you and introduce the *real you* to the rest of the world.

The real you is not small. The real you is not weak. The real you is not paralyzed by fear.

It's one thing to think thoughts like this. It's an entirely different thing to **feel** them to be true. So, that's the work to be done. You think the thoughts to reprogram yourself with material that can actually help you play BIG instead of spending your life playing small. Think these thoughts enough, and you will actually start believing them. And from that point forward, you will pretty much be unstoppable.

How to Become <u>Instantly</u> Attractive to the World

So what happens when you do the work required to remember that you are a powerful person?

I bet it's not too hard for you to think of someone in your life who only shows up when they want something from you. Or maybe you know someone who always needs something from you.

The Real You Is a Leader

Just take a minute and check in with yourself about how that word makes you feel. A leader? Me? If you're having thoughts like that, then you've just uncovered one of your biggest and most powerful opportunities for growth in your life and business.

The brainwashing most of us received from the "system" was all about installing a very simple idea in your brain. That idea is that being a leader is reserved for someone else – not you.

Why am I talking about all of this in a book that is supposed to be about getting clients? First, let's make an agreement. Let's forever get rid of the idea that you "get" clients. The energy there is all wrong. And by the time you're done with this book, you'll understand.

You don't "get" clients. You attract them. They will come to you. If you've never had that happen, I understand you might be a bit skeptical and that's fine. You don't have to believe yet. You just have to try it out for yourself. You'll prove it to yourself over time.

Okay, so why are we talking about being a leader in a book about client attraction? Because when you're out there trying to attract clients, the real secret to it is shifting your mind to the mind of a leader in your field.

Have you ever considered yourself a leader for your clients? My hunch is that you probably don't. But you are a leader. Just think about the clients that come to a stylist. They want to look great. Oftentimes, they don't know how to make that happen. They don't even know what to ask for sometimes. They depend on your ability to see what is possible for them and then to help them make that a reality. That's the description of a leader.

But until you FEEL like a leader, accept the responsibility that comes with leadership, and make your intention to lead known when you meet a new client, you'll never realize the power that comes from this.

The real you is not small. The real you is not weak. The real you is not paralyzed by fear.

People want to be led. They need to be led. They know where they're at, but they don't know how to get where they want to go!

That's why one of the big secrets to attracting a steady stream of clients is to completely transform yourself into another type of service provider. Once you do this, you're never going to think of yourself as a "stylist" again. So let's get started....

The brainwashing most of us received from the "system" was all about installing a very simple idea in your brain. That idea is that being a leader is reserved for someone else — not you.

2

YOU, THE TRUSTED ADVISOR

When you think of a "trusted advisor," what picture comes to mind? Some people might think of a favorite relative or maybe a parent. Some people might think of a lawyer or a doctor or maybe even a leader at church.

I bet I could count on the fingers of my right hand the number of people reading this book who hear the word "trusted advisor" and think of a hair stylist. Not many.

If you want your future to be one where you are able to attract a steady stream of **great** clients, then becoming a trusted advisor is one of the secrets that you will put to use.

In the last chapter I talked about how to become attractive to potential clients by becoming a leader in your area. This is something that first begins in **your head.** When you choose to commit to that path, those thoughts then affect your actions. Pretty soon, you're taking actions consistent with ones that a leader would take. When people look in from the outside, what they see is you, a leader.

But, there's an important ingredient in leadership that a lot of people don't think about. You can only become a leader in your work if people trust you.

Think how you feel when you walk onto a used car lot. You know you're about to be hunted down by some scrappy guy who looks like he just woke up and put on some clothes he's been wearing for the past two months. Your "skeptical meter" is in the red zone and you're on high alert.

This is the opposite of trust. You know you can't trust anyone to do anything in your own best interest. This is a car lot, remember! They only care about one thing. They care about selling you a car – pretty much at any cost.

Now car salespeople aren't bad people, but they are doing something pretty dumb when they act like this. After all, the only reason you **don't** trust them is that you've been trained by them NOT to trust them. It's actually pretty simple.

The Golden Rule Works!

"Do unto others as you would have them do unto you...." It's pretty simple yet difficult at the same time. This is the rule you follow if you want to earn the status of trusted advisor with your prospective clients and long-time clients. Your future in the hair business depends on the

number of people that trust you to do what is in their best interest over and over again.

So, at this point, if this whole idea of earning the role of "trusted advisor" is new to you, I imagine you might be thinking, *"Hey Marquetta, don't you think this is a little much? Trusted advisor? We're just hair stylists. It's not like we're doctors or lawyers or anything."*

If you've got thoughts like that running through your head, I have two things to say that **you need to hear**.

....

You can only become a leader in your work if people trust you.

....

First of all, never EVER disrespect the value that you bring to this world. This is not about being humble. It's about avoiding the self-sabotage that keeps people small. And thinking of yourself as "just a hair stylist" is just one of the clues that you have that self-sabotaging programming living in your mind.

So, I recommend you never again allow the words, *"I'm just a hair stylist…"* **ever** be allowed to live in your mind again.

If you want clients who pay high fees without even blinking an eye, then you need to walk around understanding (and being a champion for) the true value that you bring to your clients' lives.

You're Not a Lawyer or a Doctor?
You "Just" Style Hair? <u>Thank God!</u>

People go to lawyers and doctors because they **have** to go to those people. They generally go there because they have a legal problem or health need. These are <u>not</u> pleasant experiences.

But your clients come to you, the hair stylist, because they **WANT** to come. They **want** to look much better after they leave than they did when they walked through the door. They **want** what you have because what you have adds value to their lives!

Being "the best stylist in the world" is about how you approach your work with clients. It is a frame of mind. It is a way of being and carrying yourself.

Have you ever thought about what an amazing opportunity that is to brighten someone's entire world? So please, don't ever go around thinking you are "less than" or "just a hairstylist." That's hogwash. Catch yourself when those ideas bubble up. It's not your fault. It's just that programming we talked about earlier. It wasn't put there to make you your best self. It was put there to make you easy to control.

Who Buys You First?

I heard a quote once. It was something like, *"If you wouldn't buy you, they won't either!"* Think about what that means for a second.

What that means is that the first person who must be sold on the idea that **you** are the "best stylist in the world" is YOU. If you don't believe it, why should anyone else?

But if you **do believe it…** well, hold onto your hat because that feeling is contagious. And it will make you attractive.

Please understand this idea.

Being the best stylist in the world isn't about bragging, and it's not about saying that everyone else is terrible. Being "the best stylist in the world" is about how you approach your work with clients. It is a frame of mind. It is a way of being and carrying yourself.

You **must** develop the ability to truly believe that, at that moment, you are the best choice for them in their situation in your area.

Once you install that belief, only then is it possible to truly serve someone in a way that they will remember forever.

The Recipe for Transforming Yourself into a Trusted Advisor

Why is all of this "trusted advisor" stuff so important? It's because this is something that's absolutely necessary for attracting the type of clients you want.

We're working backwards here. The goal of this book is to show you what it takes to attract hair clients on demand. We're starting by working on the most important piece of the puzzle (YOU!) and then working backwards through how you actually go out there and attract the clients. So, we'll get to the marketing part of this process – advertising how to make yourself stand out.

But, if you don't get this foundational stuff right, you're going to struggle.

So how do you become a trusted advisor as a hair stylist? Well, you ultimately have to master a skill that doesn't come so naturally to most human beings. That skill is the ability to take the spotlight off of you and put it directly on your prospects and clients.

How Do You Attract More Clients by Talking <u>Less</u> about You?

This might sound a bit crazy if you've never tried it, but it is absolutely necessary if you want to be attractive to clients. Stick with me here because what I'm about to walk you through could very easily change the future of your business all by itself. In fact, the skill you are about to learn, if you put it into practice, will completely set you apart from every other stylist out there who **doesn't** have this skill.

It all starts with understanding a simple truth about attracting clients:

Clients Don't Care about You

Sounds a little harsh, doesn't it? But it's true. Clients just don't care about you. I don't care what they say or how much they insist they **do** care. They just don't. This isn't a problem, of course. It just *is*. We're not looking for new friends here; we're looking for clients. And to attract them, you have to develop a deep understanding of what they actually want.

So, we've established clients don't care about you. They also, surprisingly, don't care about what you do. Look, if they could step into a machine, press a button, and walk out with their hair looking fabulous, they would. Wouldn't you? But for now, that's not possible.

So if clients don't care about you and they don't even care about what you do, what in the world do they care about? And why do they pay hair stylists money?

Clients Don't Care about You OR What You Do – They Only Care about What They <u>GET</u> Because of What You Do!

Think about that. Your clients are not interested in the type of scissors you use. Or the type of color you use. Or your latest weave technique. Or how quickly you can fit them in.

At the end of the day, your clients are buying the **feeling** they have when they walk out of the salon. It's the thing that makes them feel good about themselves. It's the feeling they get when their best friend says, *"Girl, you look great!"*

That's what your clients get because of you. It's all about feelings!

So you might be able to understand why discounts, and all of the other stuff stylists do to attract clients, are just dead-ends. Do you really want a client in your chair that came ONLY because she got a discount? That's not really the type of client that is going to be willing to pay double the going rate for the opportunity to sit in your chair.

So, what do your hair clients actually get because of you? Because that's what they're buying, and to the extent that you make it clear that's what you're selling, they will search you out.

Now, let's go back to the idea of taking the spotlight OFF you and putting it right on your prospective clients. When you do that and actually start talking about your clients and what they actually want, you are going to stick out in a major way.

Think about it. Most stylists just blab on and on about themselves. This is the #1 LEAST interesting topic for your clients. If you are one of those stylists who just can't stop talking about yourself – be honest with yourself – just understand that this is the exact OPPOSITE thing you need to be doing to attract clients.

I make a big deal about this because, ultimately, we are in a business of service. And one of the most valuable skills you can develop to be successful is the ability to put yourself in the shoes of your prospective clients. Try it. View the world from your clients' perspective. How do they feel? What are they thinking about? What do they want? What are they afraid of? These are all extremely valuable things to think about.

Again, this isn't about **you.** It's about **them.** And once you get clued into that and start practicing it, people are going to notice. They will be attracted to you because you'll make it obvious that you are interested in their favorite subject: THEMSELVES!

At the end of the day, your clients are buying the feeling they have when they walk out of the salon.

So to be sure that you know this first secret – that you need to talk about what your clients GET, not just what you do – let's move on to the next step in transforming you into a trusted advisor.

The Needy Service Provider

Think of that person in your life who always needs something from you. Every time you see them, they walk away after having asked you for something. Maybe it's to borrow a few dollars or maybe it's to listen to them talk about themselves. Maybe they just come to you so you can tell them what a good person they are. ☺ That gets old, doesn't it? Can't you just feel it coming when that person approaches? You might be too nice to say anything, but you know the feeling. It's that "Oh, boy, here we go again…" feeling that makes you want to pretend you didn't see this person coming.

That's what happens to the world around you when you go through your day in a state of need.

What in the world does this have to do with attracting clients? Well, it has everything to do with attracting clients. And if you think back to the scenario I just went through about that "needy" person in your life, then you can already feel why.

Neediness repels. The "needier" you are, the more people will steer clear of you.

View the world from your clients' perspective.

I'm not talking just about needing money. I'm talking about need on many different levels.

We talked earlier about you assuming your rightful position as **leader** in the eyes of your clients. Well, it's hard to be an effective leader, someone who inspires people to be their best, if YOU are walking around in a state of need.

So part of becoming a trusted advisor is to develop the ability to banish "need" from every part of your life. The reason you do this is because people can feel this. And it affects them on a very deep level. They probably aren't even consciously aware of it.

What happens when you successfully banish *need* from your *being* and go through the world like that? I can tell you…. People will be attracted to you. Think about that person in YOUR life that never asks you for anything. All they ever do is help you. They give, and they give some more. They never ask for anything in return!

They will be attracted to you because you'll make it obvious that you are interested in their favorite subject: THEMSELVES!

How do you feel about a person like that? They are nice to be around, aren't they? Well, have you ever thought about the reason why? It's because they don't need anything from you!

The Biggest and Most Damaging Type of Need

We talked earlier about the "brainwashing" we all received in school. With the teacher up there in front of the classroom, we were taught to listen, to pay attention, and to do what we were told to do. If we DID that, we were rewarded. If we DIDN'T do that, we were penalized.

I'm sure the teachers in your life were well-meaning. They're just doing the best they can. But the system they had to work in wasn't created to make successful individuals. It was created to make workers.

There are a lot of problems with it. There are a lot of problems when something like that is introduced into your life.

When you don't need someone's approval or validation for the actions you take in your life, that mindset makes you instantly attractive – to others – on a deeper level.

What happens when you spend 12 years listening to a single voice of authority telling you what to do? What happens when you spend 12 years of your life having your actions graded and compared with others?

What happens when you are told over and over again that there's a right answer and a wrong answer to everything?

What happens is that when you step into the real world, you start looking for someone who can fill that role of "teacher" in your life. You start looking for people to validate that what you are doing is right. You start looking for proof that other people think that what you are doing is good.

Eventually, we end up with a world that is not free. We end up with a world where everyone is controlled by what they think other people are thinking of them.

So, I'm going to be blunt. In the interest of showing you the way to becoming a master of client attraction by becoming the best version of yourself, I'm going to risk offending you.

So listen up....

You Will **Never** Reach Your Full Potential for Success In The Hair Industry If You Care What Other People Think of You

I'm serious about this. And it's especially important in the hair industry because you come in contact with a lot of big personalities. But you don't want to end up living in the prison of being controlled by all of the people outside you. This is how most people live. They are more concerned with what others think of them than they even are about what they think of themselves. It's sad, really. It makes your life miserable, so you lose twice.

You may be wondering what this has to do with attracting awesome hair clients. Well, it has everything to do with it.

And that brings us to Client Attraction Law #2....

Client Attraction Law #2:
People are Extremely Attracted to People Who Don't Care What Others Think about Them!

This makes perfect sense if you think about it. When you don't need someone's approval or validation for the actions you take in your life, that mindset makes you instantly attractive – to others – on a deeper level.

You can probably begin to understand why it actually makes sense when I say the best way to attract clients is to stop needing them. On an energetic level, "need" is repulsive to success. The only thing it attracts is others with a similar need.

So, if you're like me and have spent more than a decade of your life being taught to look to other people (the teacher!) for approval and validation, how in the world are you supposed to fix that?

The answer is that you fix it slowly. You didn't get into this mindset overnight, and it can take a little time to get out. But now that you're aware of it, you're already way ahead of most people. They don't even realize that this dynamic is running their lives.

How to Banish Need Forever and Become More Attractive to Prospective Clients

Please understand that this is worth the work, especially if you want to ramp up your ability to attract clients. Never forget that people are attracted to people who don't need them! It's crazy but it's true.

So the first step to this client attraction transformation is to become **aware** of your need for other people to like you. You know where you're at in this journey. Do you spend a lot of time caring what others are thinking of you? Do you worry about whether this client or that client "liked" what you did?

Understand that this doesn't mean you aren't out to serve your clients. That's the business we're in, so that's a given. We are there to serve. The problems start when we make our satisfaction or happiness depend on someone else's happiness. When you work on a client's hair, you know whether or not you gave it your best work. You know if you "showed-up" for them and did your best to make them look great.

What you don't control, however, is whether or not they agree with your opinion. And that's why so many hair stylists make themselves miserable without even knowing it. They make their own happiness depend on something that's outside their own control!

The first step to freeing yourself from this control is to be aware of these emotions as they come up, and then simply refuse to take the action that you've been trained to take.

We've all been trained to please the teacher but when you really think about it, serving a client requires that you raise the bar. If you are truly in this business to serve your client, then you want to put your need to feel "liked" way off to the side. Eventually, when you practice this strategy enough, it will become your new habit. It's at that point that you will be free. You will be free to serve others in the best way that you possibly can.

The benefit to doing all of this work is that you will increase the attractive force pulling clients to you. You might not believe me yet and that's okay. Just put this into practice, and I guarantee that you are going to be surprised at what happens.

The problems start when we make our satisfaction or happiness depend on someone else's happiness.

3

Dear Stylist, So Why Should We Hire You and Not Someone Else?

Eek! Don't you hate having to answer a question like that? Why should your clients hire you and not someone else? Do you have a good reason? Do you have something to tell them?

If not, then this chapter is for you. In just a few minutes, I'm going to help you discover the answer to that question. I'm going to walk you to an answer that's going to give you a lot of clarity.

Understand that it's entirely possible that no one will ever ask you this question directly. But that's not important. What is important is that you have an answer anyway. Why? Because until you do, the "signal" you send out in the marketplace to attract clients – we'll talk about this in an upcoming chapter – will not be clear.

The Power of Clarity

Let's talk for a moment about why clarity is so important. Most stylists struggle with attracting clients because they try to attract anyone and everyone. Let me put your mind at ease. Don't bother trying to attract everyone into your salon. Don't bother trying to attract all types of people. It's not worth your time. Plus, you'll only end up with the clients no one else wanted.

One of the most valuable things you can get clear is what you deliver to your clients that they can't get anywhere else. What makes you unique? What makes you the best choice for your clients?

Now, don't worry. If answers to all of these questions aren't flooding into your mind right now, that's no problem. I'm actually being a little hard on you here because these are sometimes some of the most difficult questions to answer.

Most stylists struggle with attracting clients because they try to attract anyone and everyone.

They're difficult because they're important. In the coming minutes, I'll help you to get closer to your answer than you might be right now. This is a <u>process</u>. You're not looking for a big flash to come out of the sky and give you the answers right away. The process is a little more like peeling an onion. You take off one layer at a time until you hit the center.

Why This Is Work worth Doing

If you can get some of these answers about your own work as a stylist, then it's much easier to "put that light" out into the world and attract the right clients. Understand this idea: there's only one thing worse than having ZERO clients and that's working all day with clients who have no business working with you!

When you are clear about why someone should choose YOU over and above every other stylist out there, then those are the things you talk about when you are advertising and promoting yourself.

When you **aren't** clear about any of this, then you are forced to do things to attract clients that aren't in anyone's best interest.

This is why you see stylists discounting their services so much….

This is why you see stylists afraid to "charge too much…."

This is why you see stylists almost begging for business on places like Facebook®. When you have no clarity about why a client would choose you, then the only thing that is left is to do is what everyone else is doing.

Understand that discounts, low fees, and hounding prospective clients to make an appointment with you will bring you the *worst clients* there are. You will not enjoy spending your day working with these folks. Just understand that you are in control of this problem. That's why it's so important to do some of this hard thinking. This, alone, will separate you from a LOT of other stylists.

Why Seeing These Answers Can Be So Difficult

Why do so many stylists have such a hard time figuring out what makes them unique in the marketplace? Well, some stylists have nothing unique about them simply because they are mediocre. Now that might sound harsh, and it is. But it's no harsher than the world is going to be with you.

Understand that everything I say in this book is aimed at the stylist who commits to rising above the level of average. Nothing great happens for average people. If you're reading this book, then that simple act puts you way above the average stylist already.

I want to highlight this fact because your success in this business does actually depend, in part, on your skills as a stylist. It's not everything, but it is important. So commit to being great at what you do. That makes everything else much easier.

Okay, so now that we have that out of the way, let's talk about you and why you might struggle to see what makes you a unique and valuable stylist in the marketplace.

The reason that this is oftentimes hard to see is that we have been trained to ignore it. I'll keep my cool here, but this is a terrible thing to do to a child as she grows up. Think back to your school days. What happened with the kids who "stuck out?" What happened to the kids that were different, that did things their own way? Can you remember some of those kids? We all had them.

What I remember is that those kids were called out. They were told to "get in line." They were told, "That's not how we do it." Sometimes they were actually punished. I'm not talking about the kids who tried to be trouble. I'm talking about the kids who were simply being themselves. They were being their one-of-a-kind selves in a system that couldn't tolerate that type of behavior.

Over time, those kids either got "ejected" from the system, or they submitted to the system. Like I said, it's terrible.

Most all of us were subjected to training like this. This is why so many kids in school spend so much time and energy trying to be like the other kids. School was designed to train the "uniqueness" out of you. That works if you're going to spend the rest of your life in an office job somewhere, just punching the time clock.

But if you're going to be in business for yourself – if you're going to make your own way in the world – then this training is something you want to get rid of ASAP because it's hiding from you the GOLD that is going to become the foundation of your success.

Does This Really Matter in the Real World?

Does all of this really matter in the real world? Are any of these ideas going to contribute to you doubling – or even tripling – your income in the hair industry?

Well, let me ask you a question. Have you ever discounted your services for a client when they asked? Have you ever discounted your services for a client BEFORE they asked because you were afraid they'd go somewhere else?

Is there a reason you don't charge double your rate for your current services? Have you ever thought about why you charge what you charge?

Now I don't know you, but my hunch is that stylists who charge what everyone else is charging do it for two reasons.

The first reason is because that's what everyone else charges. The second reason is because stylists don't think anyone would choose them if they doubled their rates.

And you know what? That might be right. If you doubled your rates today, your current clients might choose not to pay them… but other clients would. Those are the type of clients who pay those kinds of fees for styling services.

What Happens to the Value of Something When It Is One of a Kind?

So, here is where we start to turn the corner. I want to show you just how much of your potential is untapped right now. Let me start with a question, and I'll make it about one of my favorite topics: fashion!

What happens when a high-end designer creates a purse and puts it out on the market? Let's say they decide to make only 1,000 of them per year. Once those are sold, that's it.

> *When you are clear about why someone should choose YOU over and above every other stylist out there, then those are the things you talk about when you are advertising and promoting yourself.*

If the designer is well-known, those 1,000 purses aren't going to last long. They won't be cheap, but price will hardly matter to the buyers. *They want the purse.* And because the supply of them is so much less than the demand for them, the designer can pretty much name any price.

As Demand for Something Exceeds Supply of That Something, Prices Go Up!

This is an enormous clue to explain why so many stylists are working for peanuts. From the perspective of their clients, there is nothing special about stylist X that the client can't get from stylist Y. That's when you have **downward** pressure on fees. You go to stylist X and say, *"Hey, Stylist Y is willing to do this for $XX… can you beat that?"*

If you've ever been in a position like that, you know it's terrible.

Let me make it really plain for you: if you can figure out how to make YOURSELF a "one-of-a-kind" stylist, you are going to see everything about your work improve: the fees, the respect, the way your clients talk, and the way they think about you. EVERYTHING.

But, you have to take a look at the clues about what makes you that "one-of-a-kind" stylist and then communicate that message to the world.

So, let's get to work....

The 3-Step Process to Becoming a One-of-a-Kind Stylist

Okay, we're going to do this one step at a time. And the first thing you want to realize is that if you're going to become a "one-of-a-kind" stylist, you have to figure out for who you are going to do that. Like I touched on before, you can't be the perfect choice for everyone. You can only be the perfect choice for a certain type of person. *(We're actually going to go through some of this process TWICE, so even if you can't get some of your answers right away here, you'll get another chance soon. You'll see why....)*

Step 1: Who Are We Talking About?

Step 1 is figuring out what your ideal client actually looks like. Who is this person? Where does he/she live? What does he/she like to do? What are his/her fears? What are his/her dreams? Get out some paper and a pen and start to write this down. Write down everything you know about this person. What we're really after is a clear understanding of what makes this person tick.

When you understand who you are trying to attract, you know what to say and how to say it so it resonates with that type of person.

Step 2: What Pain Do You Relieve?

Now that you are getting a clearer picture of your ideal client, the next step is to get a feeling for what type of "pain" this person is in when it comes to the services you provide. Now we're not doctors here, so when I say "pain" I'm not talking about someone with a concussion or a broken limb. That's one kind of pain, but that's not the one we're after.

Maybe you've never thought about it, but as a stylist you DO relieve a type of pain for your clients. It's the pain that comes from being self-conscious about how they look. Or the pain that comes from them not looking their best. Or the pain they experience when they know their look is one or two generations "behind the times."

Just think about it. We're talking about EMOTIONS here. That's what drives people to buy products and services.

School was designed to train the "uniqueness" out of you.

Think about the car industry. No one buys a Mercedes® just to get around. An old clunker can get you from point A to point B. People buy high-end cars because of something deeper, something more powerful. They buy them because it communicates something to the world about them.

So, go back to your piece of paper. We're going to make a list of pain. Think of all of the pain that would cause your client to call a stylist, to make an appointment, and to actually show up. This might take some thinking to get a long list but do your best. You might start with one or two obvious items and then not be able to think of any more. Trust me, the list can be much longer than one or two items. It just might take some work.

What you want to end up with is the longest possible list of all the types of pain that you solve for your clients. (For example, I don't want to be embarrassed by my looks in front of my friends.) Give this some time. It's going to serve as an enormous advantage for you if you do this.

What you end up with is a snapshot of why your clients invest their money in looking great. Over time, you'll expand your list, add new items, and develop a clearer understanding of what your clients actually care about.

Step 3: Thinking about *Your* Journey

The final step of the process is to go through each of those "pain" items and think about all of the other stylists you know. Now ask yourself, *"How does the journey that I take my clients on to relieve their pain DIFFER from the journey they'd take with someone else?"*

This process is a little bit like those magical picture books where you have to squint your eyes to see the hidden picture. We're kind of "reading between the lines" here.

The fact is that the service you provide to your clients IS unique. They can't get the exact same thing anywhere else. But, until you figure out HOW it's unique and understand an effective way to communicate that, well… the message just gets lost. Your clients understand what makes you unique but only AFTER they work with you.

We're trying to get clear on this so we can communicate it to prospective clients BEFORE they hire you.

What to Do While You're Figuring Out All of This

There are really two main parts to the client attraction process. Think of your business as a "radio station." You broadcast a certain signal out into the marketplace.

Part one is focusing your signal. That's what we're right in the middle of now. Part two, which we'll get to later on, is to amplify your signal.

Do you see, though, how it would be possible for a stylist to struggle if they try to grow their business without having a clear "signal" to send out into the marketplace?

The reality of the situation is even worse. Not only do most stylists have a fuzzy signal, but they also have no clear understanding about the best place to send that signal. They send it out to everyone in the world and then wonder why crowds of people aren't banging down their door.

So, now that we've done some hard thinking, I have really good news for you. I **do** want you to spend some time thinking about all of this, but the good news is that you don't have to get this part all figured out before you see real results in your business.

Most stylists have no idea this level of client attraction even exists. So, the simple act of reading this book puts you way ahead of the pack. And when it comes to setting yourself apart from every other stylist out there, I'm going to give you a shortcut to doing that in just a little while. It's not "thinking." It's actually doing. And it's kind of a shortcut to get your clients to tell you what makes you unique and valuable to them. That way, you don't even have to work hard to figure it out! The secret is…

Think of your business as a "radio station." You broadcast a certain signal out into the marketplace.

4

THE POWER OF THE PLATFORM!

The secret is something called the Platform. Think back to the days when Oprah was on TV every afternoon. How did she build such an enormous following of people who liked her, trusted her, and took her advice?

She did it by showing up in the lives of her viewers day after day, year after year, decade after decade! That's a long time. And if you were one of the people who watched her show, my hunch is that you probably felt like you "knew" her in some way.

There's something magical that happens when someone shows up as promised for an extended length of time. If they have a message that resonates with the world, a deep bond is formed. Relationships are created and then, with time, strengthened.

If you ask the average stylist about how to get clients, most of them will just give you a blank stare. They simply don't know the first step to take to go about getting clients in the door. Look, I went to cosmetology school. That's definitely **not** something they teach you how to do there. It's kind of funny, actually. You develop the skill and ability to take on hair clients, and you walk out into the real world lacking the #1 skill required to make that happen.

Some stylists have figured out a thing or two that allows them to get clients. But here's where my view differs from what you'll see out there. You see, I think "attracting clients" is something that you are doing all of the time.

If you remember nothing else from this section of the book, remember this truth about the hair industry: the worst time to try to get clients is when you actually need clients.

It's kind of funny, really. But, it's not funny if it's your reality. When I opened my salon, I never had a problem attracting clients. Now I didn't want to stand behind a chair all day, every day, so I limited my available time. Even so, attracting clients was never a problem. Why?

Because I didn't start attracting clients when I needed them. I started attracting them LONG ago.

Avoiding a Sure Path to Insanity

Someone once said that insanity is doing the same thing over and over again and expecting a different result each time. I guess that's one definition of insanity. But I have another one for you – another one that's a whole lot more practical in the real world.

I think insanity is when you focus energy *on* or stress *about* things that are outside of your control. Sadly, this is what most people do most of the waking hours of their lives.

....

There's something magical that happens when someone shows up as promised for an extended length of time. If they have a message that resonates with the world, a deep bond is formed.

....

They freak out about things that are outside of their control. There are two problems with that. First, it's extremely tiring and stressful, and it leaves you feeling like a helpless and hopeless individual. The second problem is worse. If you spend your days worried about things outside of your control, that doesn't really leave much time to invest in doing things that **are** within your control.

So what does this have to do with getting clients? Well, it has *everything* to do with it.

The Harsh Reality: You Don't Control Whether a Client Chooses to Sit in Your Chair or Not

That sounds a little bleak doesn't it? If you don't control whether or not you get clients, then why even bother? And what are we doing here going through all of this together?

Well, let's go back to my definition of insanity. At this point we know we can't ultimately control whether or not clients choose to hire us and get their hair done. So, now that we **know** that, we can stop freaking out about it.

Have you ever watched a stylist try to **convince** someone to make an appointment? It's sad to watch. In fact, it makes you feel sorry for everyone involved. You feel sorry for the stylist because she's obviously desperate for clients, but you also feel sorry for the client because it feels terrible to be pressured like that. And it's certainly not going to create a positive impact on how that client views the stylist.

My recommendation to you right now is to stop trying to get clients. You read that right. Stop investing energy, and focus on something you do not control. Instead, we're going to focus all of that energy on something you actually **do** control, something that will actually bring the clients without you trying to get them! We're going to use "Oprah's Secret" to attract clients to your salon.

Put On Your Platform Shoes!

The secret is the Platform. What is it? It can be a lot of things. For Oprah, it was her TV show. For me, it's a podcast, videos, emails, and more. Even this book! For you, it could be a newsletter, a video blog, an audio/video podcast, or something else. Before we get to what your Platform looks like, let's talk about why it works and what makes it so valuable.

Attracting clients is not a one-time event. Like I said earlier, you don't attract clients when you need them; you attract clients all the time!

Before a client decides to come to your salon and sit in your chair, a few things have to be true:

#1: They Must Know You Exist
#2: They Must Know You Are Skilled
#3: They Must Trust You

So, how do you go about making sure those things happen? Well, you can't really just come out and say it. Stylists who do that just end up being annoying. Needing to "convince" a client that you are awesome makes you look NOT awesome.

The answer to my question is the Platform. The Platform is what communicates all of these things to your prospective clients over time. The Platform is a DEMONSTRATION tool. Think back to Oprah again.

If you've ever seen her on TV or even on the Internet, what is she doing? Well, some people would watch and say, *"She's a great interviewer...."* That would certainly be one obvious answer, but it's more than that. What she's actually doing is providing a **demonstration** of what she is about. Day after day... more demonstration. Eventually, you begin to trust someone like that. Eventually, you begin to see just how skilled and talented that person is. Eventually, you realize that this person is for you!

The Platform Is All about Demonstration

If you read any book on sales or marketing, it won't take you long to find one that explains that one of the most powerful ways to sell anything is through demonstration. Why do you think you see all of those infomercials on TV have someone demonstrating how effectively the "goop" they are selling gets stains off a countertop? DEMONSTRATION.

Now your Platform is not going to demonstrate you standing there styling someone's hair, so don't think that's all it's about.

Yes, your clients are going to come to you because they are attracted to the way you style hair. But that's just the beginning. There are plenty of competent stylists out there who can style hair.

When you use your Platform to consistently demonstrate who you are and what you're about over and over again, your prospective clients develop a relationship with YOU. They don't develop a relationship with another stylist. It's with YOU.

That means they are coming for YOU. That's the true power of the Platform. It will slowly and gently completely separate you from every other stylist out there.

Before we walk through the process to create **your** client attraction Platform, I want to close the loop on our quick discussion about insanity.

Remember, I said my definition of insanity was stressing over things you don't control. And I recommended focusing your energy and awareness only on things you DO control.

That's your Platform. You control 100% of what goes into that. And that's something that will never change. You are in complete control of it. And that means it's a worthy thing in which to invest time and energy.

When your Platform is up and running, you can stop focusing on GETTING CLIENTS – your Platform will do that – and you can start focusing on being as valuable to your prospective clients as you possibly can.

It's truly freedom to see your business like this because you will wake up each day and know what to do to move your forward. You won't be stuck wondering, *"What can I do next to get some clients?"*

The Platform vs. "Advertising"

Don't you hate it when you're watching something on TV or online, and right at the best part it cuts to commercial? Kind of annoying, isn't it, to be interrupted like that?

Well, that's how your prospective clients feel when you "advertise." Imagine how well it would go if you cut into their TV shows with a message about why they should call your salon. What if you did that six times during their show? That would surely annoy people, wouldn't it? Wouldn't it annoy YOU if someone did that?

Well, that's the general feeling people get with advertising done poorly. It's an interruption. It's annoying. And it tries to force someone to focus on something they weren't thinking about.

....

I think insanity is when you focus energy on or stress about things that are outside of your control.

....

And these days, with free tools available for every stylist with a heartbeat to make noise online, it's far worse than ever. So, what that means is that "showing up" like everyone else with coupons and discounts and normal "advertising" is just going to get you ignored.

The Platform is the complete opposite. Imagine if you had a big list of prospective clients that actually looked FORWARD to getting your "advertising?" What if they actually THANKED you for it? That can happen. It certainly happens for me… a lot.

And every time that happens, I know that it's working. I'm adding value to the lives of prospective clients, and I am being thanked for it. Everyone wins!

Before we get really specific, there's just one more Platform-related benefit I want to highlight. We talked earlier about you assuming the role of the "trusted advisor" with your prospects and clients. Well, it's hard to do that with "advertising." Shouting "Hire me! Hire me!" doesn't make you look like an advisor. It makes you look like a salesperson.

And if that's the perception your prospects and clients have of you, then you've already kind of lost. Because they will be aware that, ultimately, you are looking out for YOU and not for them. And when that trust is compromised, it's only a matter of time before they go somewhere else.

The Platform attracts clients by demonstrating that you are worthy of trust, respect, and premium fee levels. It does it slowly (don't expect overnight miracles!) and it does it consistently. Best of all, it communicates all of these things without you ever having to really say them!

How to Create Your Client Attraction Platform Blueprint in Six Minutes (or Less!)

I'm going to walk you through what is probably the world's quickest crash course in creating a Platform that will serve as the foundation of your client attraction system. You can go deep with this, but we're going to blow through it to give you a quick start. We're going to be reusing some of the same steps we did before. This second pass through should give you more clarity than the first time.

STEP 1: Double Check Your Target (Your Second Chance!)

I have to warn you. The first step in this process might be a bit of a challenge. It's going to require a commitment that many stylists probably aren't willing to make. But if you're going to create a Platform that actually works, you can't skip this step.

Platforms are not made to attract every type of client. They are made to attract a specific type of client. It's actually quite natural if you think about it. If you showed up at a party with 100 other stylists in the room you'd end up getting along with some, but you wouldn't really get along with others.

No one person is for everyone. In fact, if everyone DOES like you out there in the world, then my guess is that you probably don't stand for anything real. Because if you did, you'd be a polarizing figure. Some people would like you but many would not.

Attracting clients is not a one-time event. Like I said earlier, you don't attract clients when you need them; you attract clients all the time!

When you are attracting clients, this same dynamic is going to play out. The clearer you are about who you are and what you do and do <u>not</u> do, the easier it will be to separate the clients who you should work with from those you shouldn't.

The Platform is a DEMONSTRATION tool.

In order for the Platform to work, get clear on the type of client you want to be working with. Is she a 45-year-old woman? Is he a 24-year-old guy? We covered this briefly a little while ago, but now it's time to get serious about it.

Now, before you answer this question, think about how you want your life and your business to look. If you're looking for a certain lifestyle that you'd like to support, you have to be smart about choosing the clients that can help you do that.

If you're going for a life of luxury, filling your days with 24-year-old male clients probably isn't going to cut it. The resources most 24-year-olds have to invest in how they look are pretty limited.

My point is that you need to be realistic. More importantly, you want to be strategic. Strategic means doing things on purpose because of where you want to go.

The average stylist is in no danger of doing anything strategic. And that's why it's such a hard road that pays so poorly. Without the right strategy, all you're going to do is wake up every day and work hard. It'll never stop.

But understand that you can't put crappy ingredients in a "cake" and expect to get something that tastes amazing. Same thing with clients. If you want a certain result, you need to use the right ingredients in your recipe.

So, the first step in this Platform puzzle is to get as clear as you can right now about **WHO it is you want to attract.** If your answer is "everyone," go back and reread this section. You didn't get it.

STEP 2: Stepping into Their Shoes

Once you choose a type of client you want to be working with, get really clear on that person. You want to understand them at a very deep level. You don't have to have it all together right away. This is a process that you'll start and continue for as long as you want clients.

PICK ONE INDIVIDUAL that represents your ideal client and picture that person in your mind. What makes them tick? What do they love? What are their dreams? What scares them to death? What's the REAL reason they invest so much attention into how they look? Is it about feeling good about themselves? Are they looking to impress their friends?

Really get a clear picture of this person. This is the person we're going to build your Platform for. You want to get a clear picture of them on the level of feeling. People buy based on feelings. If you think back to some of the purchases you've made over the years, ask yourself what actually made you buy? I bet that in just about every case we could trace your motivation back to a FEELING.

Now, go back to that list of "pain" that you relieve for your clients. We worked on that just a little bit ago.

Put that pain in order of priority. Put the most painful things at the top. For example, if you work with cancer patients to help them restore their belief that they are BEAUTIFUL, the pain would be "feeling ugly." That's an enormous gift you offer to your client if that's the pain you relieve.

....

When you use your Platform to consistently demonstrate who you are and what you're about over and over again, your prospective clients develop a relationship with YOU.

....

Relieving pain and solving problems are why your clients buy. So the more time you commit to getting clear on this, the easier the rest will be.

STEP 3: Your BIG IDEAS

Big ideas are exciting. Big ideas get people to take action.

What does a "big idea" look like? Well, how about this: Pay close attention to what you're feeling as you read these next few sentences:

You have the power to create your life exactly as you want it to be. You have the tools you need to live a life most people only dream about. You can love your work, you can be financially free, and you can live rich on every level. You can have it <u>all</u>.

How did you feel? Did you notice a certain level of emotion rising in your gut? I know I did. What you just read there in bold are BIG IDEAS. They are exciting. They make you feel something.

Big ideas are what separate you from other choices your clients have.

Think about how you view what you do. Are there things that you "stand for" that other stylists don't get? Are there approaches you use to make your clients look great that other stylists don't know about?

Maybe your thing is helping women "go natural." Maybe you truly believe THAT is how we are meant to be. That's a big idea. That's something you can stand for. That's something that will surely be LOVED by many and probably HATED by just as many.

Another example might be that special process you've developed over the years that absolutely NAILS the color when you do your clients hair.

When you're thinking about what type of a Platform to create *(remember, it's a blog, or a newsletter, podcast, or some other regularly repeating publication of some kind)*, we're looking for 1-3 of these BIG IDEAS that kind of summarize what you stand for and what your clients can expect to get from you that is DIFFERENT than what they'll get from another stylist.

When your Platform is up and running, you can stop focusing on GETTING CLIENTS – your Platform will do that – and you can start focusing on being as valuable to your prospective clients as you possibly can.

If you're not used to thinking like this, this section might be confusing at first. Big ideas? What?

Don't worry if that's your best response right now. Like I said, this is a process. This is what most stylists are never told. This is a LONG-TERM plan, not a silver bullet route to overnight success.

If there was a way for overnight success in the hair industry, we'd all be doing it by now!

So, let's get back to the task at hand – getting extremely **strategic** about the message we're going to send out into the world. There's that word again – strategic. Ask the average stylist to tell you about her strategy for attracting clients, and you'll probably just get a blank stare. That *should* be a clue to you. The average stylist is completely overworked and underpaid. But that's only because they're executing on a strategy they didn't even know they had! They're executing on a strategy the industry set up, not one they set up. Those two things are completely different.

Imagine if you had a big list of prospective clients that actually looked FORWARD to getting your "advertising." What if they actually THANKED you for it? That can happen. It certainly happens for me... a lot.

Look, you're reading this book to completely transform your business and your life. I'm not pulling ANY punches. I'm going to give you the truth straight up – exactly like I see it and have lived it.

If you want to end up living a life that is WAY above average, you need a strategy to get you there. That's what I've got, and that's what I'm sharing with you.

When you use better "ingredients," you'll create better outcomes.

What Are These Big Ideas For?

Why do we need these ideas? Why am I giving you a headache by taking you through all of this hard *thinking* work?

When you finally select 1-3 "big ideas," you are going to use the content in your Platform to demonstrate these ideas over and over again. Over time, the prospective clients who subscribe to your Platform will begin to get "what you're about."

You'll basically be answering the "why should they choose YOU" question, slowly, over time.

You know what the best thing is about this "Platform" approach to client attraction? The best thing is that you don't even have to get it all right. In other words, you can screw up a lot of it and it'll still work!

Over time, you'll smooth out the areas and fix your mistakes, but you don't have to have it all perfect before you get started. Like I said, this is the exact opposite of "advertising." If you screw up a big advertisement you buy in a local newspaper or magazine, you don't get a second chance!

STEP 4: Name, Format, and Frequency

Guess what? This step is EASY. It's easier, but in this step of our journey it is actually one of the most powerful secrets of the Platform approach to client attraction.

The secret is <u>consistency</u>. Take a look at your own life for a moment. How many people in your own life "show-up" for you, without fail, as promised?

If you're like most people, your list probably isn't too long. I'm talking about someone you just KNOW is going to be there as promised.

....

Platforms are not made to attract every type of client. They are made to attract a specific type of client.

....

What's the byproduct from someone making a promise to you and then actually delivering on that promise? And what happens if that person does the same thing over and over again? What you get is trust. The byproduct of making a promise and following through is **trust**.

So, think about this. Most other stylists are going to be out there in the marketplace basically shouting, "Me, me, me!" They won't get a whole lot of attention with that approach, but that's all they know to do.

You, on the other hand, are going to approach things quite differently. You'll have your Platform. Your Platform sends valuable information into the lives of your prospective clients over and over again. This information might be instructive or empowering or even inspiring.

Sometimes you'll teach them about hair care or reveal a styling "trick" they can use. Other times you'll share a story about a transformation you helped a client undergo. Still, other times, you'll just send something uplifting that makes your subscriber feel better about herself.

Your Platform might show up every day or every week or even every month. That frequency isn't nearly as important as the consistency. And why is consistency so important? It's not because your prospective clients need more information. It's because when they said, "Yes! Add me to the list!" you made a promise that you would show up on a certain schedule.

And when you deliver on that promise, you show them that they can trust you. You might think it's not a big deal. But over time, it's a HUGE deal. Because the consistency of your Platform communicates that you are the real deal, and you never even have to say it. You just PROVE IT.

The next piece of the Platform puzzle is what to name your Platform. You give names to your services and products. There's no reason your Platform shouldn't have a name. In fact, it really must have a name. And it's probably something you'll need to think about for a little bit.

Ideally, when you're naming anything you want people to "buy" (even if it's free), the name alone would make someone want it. Let me give you a quick example to explain what I mean.

Let's say you're selling nail polish remover, and you get to the part where you have to give your product a name. You decide to name your formula something like DX86 Nail Polish Remover. You put a big DX86 logo on the bottle and put it out for sale. That's one possibility.

....

People buy based on feelings.

....

The other possibility would be quite different. The goal this time is to name it something that immediately conveys what the user gets. So clearly, DX86 doesn't cut it.

But a name like **"2-Second Polish Be Gone"** DOES work. If you want to get nail polish off your nails, all you have to do is hear that name and you know it's what you need.

Names are important. They are important because they can save you a lot of work when it comes to communicating what something is about. When you are giving a name to your Platform (your newsletter, or podcast, or whatever other form of platform you choose), ask yourself this question:

How Is My Subscriber Better Off after Reading/Listening to This Than They Were Before?

That gets your mind starting to think about your Platform in terms of how it benefits the people that are getting it. That's really the secret. Remember, no one cares about you or what you do. They only care (even if they won't admit it!) about what they get **because** of what you do.

Same thing with your Platform, whatever it ends up looking like. No one cares about it. They DO care about the benefit it brings to their lives. What are some of those benefits? That gets your mind thinking about how to name it. What would you have to call it so that when your ideal client heard the name, she would say, *"That's for me!"*

I'm going to walk you through a real-world example in just a moment. First, we have two quick items to cover.

Format and Frequency

What format should your Platform show up in (print, email, audio) and how often should you publish it?

All of these answers depend on who you are trying to attract. Chances are that the 24-year-old male client we were talking about earlier is going to be reachable in different ways than a 55-year-old woman. So your answers to the format and frequency questions depend on the WHO. Who do you want to attract?

Ask yourself, how does my target client already consume information? Via email? Via something that is printed and mailed to them? In podcast form? If you're going to go to the trouble of publishing a Platform with interesting and helpful information for your prospective clients, you want it to actually get consumed. Without consumption, there's little reason to even do it.

Now, let's move on to frequency. How often are you going to show up in the lives of your prospective clients? As simple as this one is, you don't want to screw this up. One group of folks who regularly do this are insurance agents (sorry!). They clearly are not clued in on the value of using a media Platform to attract business. That's why they send out those boring corporate email newsletters to you about once every month or every three months! The email has some boring article right alongside their picture. It's kind of sad, really. They are in the same business we are in. They are in the relationship business. But it's clear they don't understand how you actually go about **building** relationships.

The answer to this question, like many others, depends on your target client and the topics covered in your Platform. Let's say you're a Realtor. You sell real estate. No one wants to hear about buying or selling a house every day of their lives. I'm not even sure a Realtor would!

....

If you want to end up living a life that is WAY above average, you need a strategy to get you there.

....

If I were selling real estate, I wouldn't create a Platform just about real estate. Instead, I'd probably create a newsletter that was for the people in the neighborhoods I wanted to serve. The newsletter would be delivered by email, probably weekly, and it would talk about all of the neat things going on in town. My goal would be to build it into THE most popular resource to find out what's going on.

I would deliver real value to prospective clients without blabbing on and on about what I do.

For format and frequency, you need to find the intersection between what works for YOU and what works for them.

What Does This Look Like in the Real World?

Allow me to walk you through how this Platform approach might play out in the world of a stylist.

Let's say you work in Richmond, VA, and your ideal client is a middle-aged woman in your town who loves getting high-end hair and beauty services. We'll call her Shandra. She is what you might call "a mover and a shaker." That means she's up on the latest trends, she is with it when it comes to technology, and she is happy and willing to invest money in herself.

You know that Shandra's goal is to simply look drop-dead gorgeous. She knows looks aren't everything, but that's not going to stop her from doing everything in her power to look great!

You aren't necessarily going to perform every service she wants, but you ARE going to earn the trusted advisor status for all things beauty. She'll come to you first!

We're going to build your media Platform right here so you can start attracting clients like Shandra.

What's It Look Like and How Often Does It Appear?

Let's start with the easy ones: format and frequency. Now, you're a busy stylist, so you aren't going to spend all your time putting your Platform together and publishing it. You've got other work to do! So we're going to show-up in Shandra's life ONCE a week.

The format is going to be email (Shandra's iPhone® was a giveaway!). So we've got a weekly email newsletter that's going to focus on WAY more than just hair. The focus is on everything someone like Shandra needs to know to stay up-to-date on the latest beauty trends and techniques for looking great.

Wrapping Your Platform in a Package That Sells!

Next up, we need some big ideas. Remember, these are the 1-3 things that kind of sum up what you are about. So let's say you're a stylist who actually bucks some of the latest trends and fads.

You are pretty firm that a classy, understated approach to beauty is the way to go. Well, there's <u>one</u> of your big ideas.

Next up, maybe you shun all of the harsh chemicals that so many stylists use these days.

You never recommend a client put something on their body that could KILL her if she ingested it. You're all about natural, classic beauty. This is why women like Shandra are attracted to you, by the way. Shandra is all about **class**.

Finally, you are committed to helping your clients look beautiful based on who they are and what they're about. That means you don't start recommending the latest Beyoncé style **just** because it's popular. Popular isn't important. What **is** important is that your client feels like she looks gorgeous. And that's a different look for everyone.

Now remember, these aren't **your** big ideas here. I'm just making all of this up to give you an example. But, if you're still not clear about what your big ideas **are**, a great place to find an answer is to ask yourself why your clients choose you. Get their help, and you'll probably be surprised at what they say.

When you are putting your newsletter together each week (it doesn't need to be long; it just needs to be helpful!), you are going to include content that demonstrates these core ideas that separate you from the crowd.

When prospective clients read this information, you're going to repel the folks that aren't like Shandra. That's just as valuable as attracting people like Shandra. You never want to waste your time with clients who aren't right for you. The Platform is going to filter, sift, and sort for you. That's what makes it so powerful!

The byproduct of making a promise and following through is trust.

What Do We Call It?

Last up, we need a name. What do we call this newsletter? How is Shandra going to be better off after she reads it than she was before?

What value is it going to add to her life, even if she never works with you? What's in it for Shandra to read this every week?

Those are the questions you want to start thinking about. Again, don't worry if the answers don't come immediately. The magic is actually in asking the questions. Once you get them out there in the open, the answers tend to appear. It's really crazy that it works this way, but it does.

So here's one possible name. This one pretty much sums up the final benefit you get....

<u>Looking Great in Richmond</u>: Everything You Need to Know About Living Beautiful!

There you have it. That's your Platform. You do that, week in, week out. You show up for your prospective clients and you PROVE to them, in advance, that you are the go-to stylist.

Now, all of this together at one time might seem overwhelming. Don't worry! You don't have to do it all at once. I really wanted to go overboard stepping you through each part of the process. Best of all, you only need to do this once! Once your Platform is created, you can just run with it!

Okay, so what comes next? What comes after you have the Platform out there doing its thing? How do you go from newsletter subscriber to actually having a client sitting in your chair? Well, that's the FUN part, so let's go!

5

TRANSFORMING TRUST INTO PAYING CLIENTS

Building trust with a group of people is a wonderful thing. Unfortunately, trust alone will not feed your family. So next up is focusing on how to connect the dots between your Platform and actual paying clients.

Think about how this is going to flow…. You'll be publishing your Platform, and people will be reading, listening to, or watching it. At some point in time, some of those people are going to say, *"This stylist really knows what she is talking about…. I need to give this person a call."*

So then what? After you've done all of the hard work to actually get a complete stranger to call you, you don't want to mess it up! So you think through what happens next NOW so you know what you are doing.

Again, we're approaching the growth of your business from a strategic point of view. We're setting the strategy, we're creating the processes, and then we execute on those things.

If you're going to go to the trouble of publishing a Platform with interesting and helpful information for your prospective clients, you want it to actually get consumed.

That keeps you from having to wake up every day and wonder what you do to get more clients or *better* clients. You'll already know, which will save you a ton of stress. You'll have your Platform and your processes for turning those subscribers into clients – or even customers who buy other things from you. (We'll get to that!)

Building an Open Door

Basically what you need is an open door from your Platform to your salon chair. It gives your clients-to-be a clear path that you've outlined to go from prospect to client.

That's how I think of it anyway. It's clear that this is NOT how most stylists approach things, so that's a huge opportunity for you. The average stylist, if they even get as far as creating a Platform, would probably put something like this at the bottom of each newsletter issue:

"Call Me to Make an Appointment!"

What's wrong with this? After all, isn't that exactly what you want? Don't you want appointments with clients? Of course you do. But there are several problems with doing something like this. The first problem is that this is what every other stylist is going to do.

Listen clearly to this simple idea. This alone could change the future of your business: If you want to be treated like a one-of-a-kind stylist and if you want to be paid like a one-of-a-kind stylist, then you can't go around acting like an average stylist. Think about that. Think about all of the things you do right now with your clients. If your clients could get that same treatment from another stylist, right there is an opportunity for you to raise the bar.

I'm going to give you an example of what that means. I'm going to print an excerpt from a letter I prepared back when I was opening my salon. I want you to read it carefully and think about what it would feel like if YOU got a letter like this in the mail. Ready? I'll see you on the other side....

****

So, why am I writing to you?

My guess is that you've probably never received a letter quite like this one (I know I haven't!), so let me explain what this is about.

Don't worry, I'm not trying to sell you anything. In fact, I don't want anything from you at all.

My reason for writing is actually the **opposite** of that.
I'm sending you this simple invitation so that...

I Can Help <u>You</u> With Your Hair, For Free!

I'm writing to offer you something I call an *Advanced Hair Analysis*. Now very few salon owners offer anything like this and I don't know of anyone around here who's doing anything like it.

During your <u>complimentary</u> 30-45 minute *Analysis*, we'll sit down and talk hair… **your** hair. You'll get my best advice on what to do (and why) to make your hair look great! I'll tell you more in just a minute.

But, don't worry, I'm not one of those "better-than-you" salon owners that throws around hair jargon just to prove I know what I'm talking about. I don't speak "hair stylist language." And I'm not out to impress you… I'm out to **help** you.

This isn't about **me**, it's about **you**.

I want to offer you something free, with no fine print, no tricks, nothing. It might be hard to believe actually. So, keep reading and I'll explain <u>why</u> I'm doing this.

You should know there *is* one catch...

The catch is that I'm only one person. I manage 4 businesses AND I have a family with 2 kids and 3 poodles. So my time at the salon is limited.

I've sent this invitation to just over 740 women in the Summerville area. And I can probably only accept about 10 or 12 new women before I have to wait list people. So if you want to take advantage of my offer for a complimentary *Advanced Hair Analysis*, you should pick up the phone right now and reserve your spot.

The phone number to my salon (you'll want to write this down somewhere safe) is (***) ***-****.

If you call and I pick-up, introduce yourself and let me know you got my letter and want to schedule your complimentary *Advanced Hair Analysis*. If my assistant picks-up the phone or you get the salon voicemail, please make sure to mention this letter and I will call you back quickly.

My salon is located at *******. I'm right beside ****** and ******. It's a simple brick building with **loads** of parking.

At this point, I want to answer a question I bet you have in the back of your mind:

"Marquetta, Why Are You Doing This? Why Are You Making This Available?"

The fact is, I **LOVE** doing this. Yes, it's great to help customers all over the world with their hair. But working one-on-one with someone is extremely rewarding for me.

Plus, I'm so excited to finally be helping the women of Summerville and surrounding areas, that I wanted to reach out, introduce myself and do something special for the community.

Now I should probably give you a warning before you consider stepping into my world. The thing is...

I Have a Habit of Making My Clients Cry!

Of course I'm talking about <u>tears</u> of <u>joy</u>. Tears that come when you look in the mirror and KNOW you look great.

It happened just the other day in fact. I had a client come in asking for lace extensions. We'll call her Denise even though that's not her real name. Now, I don't know how much you know about hair, but there **is** no such thing as lace extensions.

So, I sat down with Denise and we had an "*Advanced Hair Analysis...*" These last up to 45 minutes.

And by the time Denise left, she knew **exactly** what she should do to make her hair look great.

During **<u>your</u>** *Analysis*, we'll go through all of the options available to you. Types of hair, types of product... all of it! I help you decide which ones are for you and which ones aren't.

So back to Denise's story…

After her *Analysis*, she set-up an appointment and I went to work. By the time I was done, she was literally in tears. Completely overjoyed with how things turned out.

I already told you how great it is to help someone feel like a million dollars.

You never want to waste your time with clients who aren't right for you. The Platform is going to filter, sift, and sort for you. That's what makes it so powerful!

And it gives me goose bumps when something like this happens. The look on my client's face makes all of the years of learning, effort, experience plus the trips to LA, NYC and Atlanta (to stay on the cutting edge)… well, it makes all of that hard work totally worth it!

Denise has been handing out my cards to friends because she's **excited** about how she looks.

<u>That's</u> why I do this. For women like Denise.

What Happens If You Respond Quickly and Get An Advanced Hair Analysis Reservation

OK… so I'm really serious about this offering not lasting too long. I really have no idea how many calls I'll get. All of my available appointments for the complimentary *Advanced Hair Analysis* might be gone in a day… maybe a week… I just don't know.

So, if you're serious about your hair (like I am), then you'll want to call right away. The number to reach me personally at the salon is (***) ***-****.

Plus, with the holidays coming, and my filming schedule and everything, things are going to be busier than ever. So be sure to act fast.

During your *Analysis,* we're going to focus on you, your hair and making you look great! At the end of your *Analysis*, you'll know more than 99% of the women out there. Best of all, you'll have the confidence you need to make the right hair choices for you.

If we're a good fit and you end up wanting to schedule an appointment at the salon, great! If not, it's no problem at all. You'll <u>still</u> have all of the information we discussed during your *Analysis* to use as you wish.

There's no pressure, and no obligation at all! In fact, if I can't help you, I'll actually work with you to find the person who can.

Like I said, I'm dedicated to helping you, no matter what that means.

****

Okay, so let's dig into this. Do you see how offering something like my *Advanced Hair Analysis* might just be a whole lot more attractive than saying "call me" at the bottom of your newsletter or at the end of your podcast?

Let's talk about why this works so much better than what most stylists do to get interested prospects to come in the door. First, there's no risk for my prospect. Second, I'm beginning the relationship by **giving value first**. Third, I'm beginning the relationship by positioning myself as an advisor, NOT as someone who's waiting to make money from a new client. Fourth, I've placed a very specific opportunity in front of my prospective clients. I've explained why I'm doing it, and I've made it clear why it's in their best interest to act sooner than later.

The end result of all of this is that I can create a relationship with a new prospect without their resistance being up. Think about how you feel when you're walking down the street and someone comes up to you and says, *"Hey, do you want to buy some sunglasses?"* Probably even before you could get a word out of your mouth, your head would be shaking NO. It's almost like a reflex we all have. When we feel like someone is trying to sell us something, our shields go up.

How do you feel when you go into a doctor's office? How do you feel when the doctor is asking you a bunch of questions about what's not feeling right? Do you feel like you're sitting in front of a used car salesman? Of course not! Well, a doctor's office is a <u>business</u>, pure and simple. They exist to make money. But, it doesn't feel like that because they've gone to great lengths to assume the position of the trusted advisor.

You take their advice! Have you ever thought about the fact that most times that advice comes with a hefty price tag? Would you take advice from a used car salesman? If a used car salesman came up to you and said, *"I recommend you buy a car today. I think that's definitely in your best interest."* You'd probably laugh him off the car lot. And you should.

How to Craft an Invitation That Starts Things off Right!

Now, to be frank, I can't tell you what that thing is that you should offer to begin a relationship with new clients. It's got to be something that's interesting. It has to be something that's valuable. And it has to be something that is attractive to your prospective clients.

So, while I can't tell you exactly what your "offer," as you might call it, should be, I can recommend what it probably shouldn't be. It probably shouldn't be, *"Call Me Today to Make an Appointment!"*

To start working towards your answer, simply put yourself in the shoes of your target client. What would you have to set out in front of them to make them say, *"I want that!"*

That's the first question to ask. In that letter excerpt you just read, my choice was a type of hair analysis session. Now, what do you think happens when you sit down with someone and prove to them that you know what you are talking about? What happens when you reveal the reasons their hair is a certain way? What happens when you explain to them **why** some of the challenges they have with their hair actually happen?

A few things happen…. First, you prove that you know your stuff. Second, you bond with the prospective client. The relationship can build pretty quickly when you show them (much better than telling them) that they can trust you with their beauty.

So, now we've started things off with YOU positioned as the trusted beauty advisor in the mind of your prospective client. If you go my route and offer some sort of hair analysis, what do you think is going to happen at the end of that? What's going to happen **after** you've imagined with them about how they *could* look? They're going to say something like, *"When can you fit me in?"* Not everyone will say that, but some will, some will come back later, and some will go away knowing that you're something special. Either way, you win.

6

How to Become
the Most Interesting
Stylist in the World

Whew! We are making enormous progress. I have to tell you, it took me a long time to piece together all of the stuff you are reading right now. There was a lot of trial and error, a lot of "wandering around" trying to figure things out, and plenty of frustration as I learned what works and what doesn't work when it comes to client attraction.

Understand that this book can save you from so much of that. Sure, you'll make your own mistakes, and you'll experiment in your own ways. Some things will work out great and others will bomb. Please understand that **this** is normal.

What you learned in school about always trying to be "right" is <u>not</u> normal. That's not how the real world works. Yes, that's how the world works if you're going to spend your life locked away in some office cubicle somewhere taking orders. But, that's not the path we're on here. We're on the path of taking what you do well and your love of hair and beauty and using it to live an amazing life.

So a few bumps and bruises along the way doesn't mean you're struggling. It means you're actually in danger of learning something real! And that's what's going to separate you from the crowd very quickly – your willingness to be confident, to be bold, to be who you are meant to be out in the OPEN.

Now, it's time to take it up a level. You've got your Platform, you're growing a list of prospective clients who like you, trust you, and are receiving helpful information from you on a regular basis. And now you have that attractive "invitation" that brings them from your Platform one step closer to becoming a client.

What Do You Do When They Actually Show Up?

If all of this Platform and mindset work hasn't already put you in a class of ONE, then what we're about to cover surely will. I'm about to give you the secret to transforming yourself into the "most interesting stylist in the world." And the best part is, you can do this right away!

So, let's talk about the average stylist. Again, this isn't what we're aiming for, of course, but it's a good reminder of how you don't want to be. Average behavior creates average results. And I want a whole lot MORE than that for you.

If you want to be treated like a one-of-a-kind stylist and if you want to be paid like a one-of-a-kind stylist, then you can't go around acting like an average stylist.

Let's say you're at a party and the room is full of a bunch of hair stylists. I bet it's not too hard for you to picture the one who just can't stop talking about herself! On and on she goes, just rambling and rambling about all of the great things she is doing – dropping names left and right of the important people she knows – doing her best to make sure **you** know that she's something special.

Ugghhh…. When I encounter people like that, I do my best to give them a nice smile and then I run for the hills! Because listening to someone like that is just tiring. You can't even get a word in. It's just like someone opened up a fire hose and directed it straight at you. Eek!

How to Control Any Conversation and Make Yourself Look Awesome!

When it comes to attracting clients into your life, you have to understand that the force of attraction is controlled by whether or not they like being around you. Sounds obvious, but most people don't do anything about it.

When you're speaking with a prospective client, there's an extremely simple way to take control of the conversation (not in an annoying way) and to come out looking like the most interesting stylist in the world.

The secret is to give up talking about yourself and start talking about your client's number one favorite subject: HERSELF!

This is a little bit counter-intuitive, but it's exactly how the real world works. So, pay close attention here. You would *think* that the way to impress someone would be to make sure they are clear about everything you can do, all of your experience, and all of your qualifications. As it turns out, however, this is exactly the wrong way to go about becoming attractive to prospective clients.

The reason why goes back to what we were talking about earlier in the book: no one cares about you. People care about themselves.

So, the skill you want to develop is the ability to take the "spotlight" off of you and shine it directly on your prospective client.

The way you do this is by asking questions.

In any conversation, the person that is in control is the one who is asking the questions. The question asker can take the conversation in any direction. The question asker can probe for more information. The question asker can get more clarification about things that aren't clear.

The funny part is that the question asker is the one who ends up adding most of the value to the conversation!

This is how you can spend 20 minutes talking with a prospective client, barely say ANYTHING, and have them walk away thinking what an interesting person you are. If I hadn't experienced this in my life, I probably wouldn't believe it.

I'm not asking you to trust me. I'm asking you to try it out and see what happens!

All Questions Are <u>Not</u> Created Equal

Before you put this tool to use, there are a few important things to know. First of all, in order to become a trusted advisor to your clients, you have to have the information required to help them make smart decisions. To GET the information, you need to ask. So "asking questions" is actually going to be something you practice for the rest of your life.

It won't take you long to become a master, though, and you'll soon realize (even if you're starting at the beginning) just how valuable and powerful this skill is.

The first rule of thumb is to banish (almost forever) any question that can be answered by your prospect with a "Yes" or a "No."

Asking Yes or No questions creates dead-ends. "Do you want color?" "Are you happy with your hair?" Answers to these questions minimize the amount of information you are going to receive. At this stage of the game, you want **more** information, not less.

The extremely powerful questions, the ones that are going to turn you into an **advisor**, cannot be answered with "yes" or "no."

For example, what happens when you're on the phone with a prospective client and you ask something like, *"Why don't you tell me about the biggest obstacles you think are standing between you and looking your best?"*

Now, that's a valuable question because when your prospect answers it, you're going to get a ton of valuable information about the "pain" your prospect is currently feeling. This is the pain you solve. But you can't solve it without knowing what it is and, more importantly, without knowing how your prospect thinks about it.

Next up, another question. ☺ You'll find that one question leads into another and then another. This is fine. You might feel weird asking all of these questions, but you'll get over it.

Think about a visit to the doctor from the past. This is exactly what the doctor does. The doctor asks questions. Sometimes the doctor asks LOTS of questions. *"Where does it hurt?" "How long has this been bothering you?" "What happens when you do X? What happens when you do Y?"* Doctors are full of questions. Why? Because without questions, they can't get answers. And without answers they can't develop a targeted solution JUST for you.

This is the very same role you can take with your clients. Trust me, **very** few stylists view themselves this way. Most stylists view themselves as "vendors." Vendors are order takers. The client comes in and the client says, *"I want you to do X, Y, Z...."* Then the stylist does it. That's not an advisor; that's a vendor. And it's not the way to go. If you go through your life as a "vendor," there will only be two questions you will get asked: *"How much do you charge? How quickly can you get me in?"*

Here's another question for you to put into your toolbox. This one will tell you just about everything you need about what your prospective client actually wants. Now I didn't make this one up, but frankly, I can't remember where I heard it. The question is something you ask fairly early in the discussion:

Can You Describe to Me What Your Picture of "Success" from Our Work Together Looks Like?

Now, you might need to help your prospective client here a bit. This might be the first time that they are thinking about describing themselves looking great as "success." But it's really not a difficult thing. This is a powerful question because this question should really get your prospect talking. She will start talking about what she truly wants. This is what you need to hear!

Most stylists are what I call "solutions in search of problems to solve." In other words, stylists START the conversation with what they are going to do. They start with the prescription. They completely skip over the "diagnosis." Think about what a doctor does. The doctor doesn't just hand you a bottle of pills after saying, "Hi." The doctor spends time in the diagnosis phase of things. He has to figure out what the proper course of action is.

This is what you're going to do, as well.

You figure out where they want to go. You figure out what they feel is standing in the way. Then you propose one (or several) courses of action.

Can you imagine how much you are going to stick out (in a GOOD way) if you start acting like this?

So, you're asking all these questions, really getting clear, and helping your client get clear on the right way to go. Then what? How do you "close the deal" and get a client?

Well, you might think that in order to succeed as a stylist and to become a highly paid stylist, you'd have to become a great salesperson. But that's not true. In fact, it's about the opposite of what is actually true.

If you can become a master at asking your prospects and clients the right questions, you will find that they pretty much sell themselves on working with you. And wouldn't **you** want to work with you when you assume the role of a trusted advisor? Of course you would. How many places could your clients go and get treatment like this? The answer is very few. And that's why this is such an amazing opportunity for you. Because if **you** become the stylist in your area that's providing service like this, word will get around.

Your Goal is <u>Not</u> to Sell!

Advisors don't sell. Advisors advise. This is a very different feeling from the perspective of your client.

Think about the last time you were "sold" on something. You could feel that the salesperson wanted you to do something. Maybe you could feel them trying to control you so that you would buy what was being sold.

How did that feel? It doesn't feel good. And the harder they push, the more you resist. Now this is NOT what you want your prospects and clients feeling about you. This is why my approach to client attraction pretty much takes "selling" off the table. You don't have to do it. Instead, you're going to create opportunities where your clients want to buy YOU!

The minute you feel like someone is trying to sell you something, your defenses go up. You get a little bit skeptical; you start wondering what the "catch" is.

This is not how you want your prospective clients feeling.

Therefore, after you collect all of your information, present options for moving forward. Sometimes it works really well to give your prospective clients a choice of options. That way, you are presenting them with a "take it or leave it" feeling.

Then wait for them to make a choice. Practice not caring about what that choice is. In fact, you want to develop the ability to truly not care whether or not they decide to work with you.

The secret is to become a master at asking questions.

7

REWRITING YOUR MONEY PROGRAMS AND CHARGING PREMIUM FEES

This chapter is a big one because there's really no area of our lives that is more screwed up (on purpose!) than our relationship with money. Some people say money is evil; some people treat it like their own God. Some people have no clue why they can't get any, and other people are all but drowning in it.

Now, I had to overcome some serious money issues as my business has grown over the years. You might not think that figuring out how to do what you love AND make a lot of money would be a problem. Doesn't everyone want that? Everyone says they do, but their actions and thoughts are not consistent with that. That's the beginning of why we have so many problems in and around the area of money.

The Energy of Money

The first step is to stop thinking about money as a thing. I know it might look like a thing and even feel like a thing, but it's not a thing. Thinking of it like that will work against you.

Money is energy. The reason you want to think about it that way is because money acts according to the laws of energy, not the laws of material things. That's why so few people understand it. That's why it's so hard to get when you need it. That's why so many people get frustrated when they wake up one morning and find they don't have any.

The fact is, everything is energy. So when you learn the rules about how energy works and about how to use it to your advantage instead of having it work against you, everything flows better.

You learn these rules **once,** and the benefits ripple through just about every area of your life.

Energy and Client Attraction

So, let's talk about energy and client attraction for just a moment. When you become a master of client attraction, you are learning to manipulate energy. Think about it…. The absolute worst way to get clients is to stand out on the street corner and ask for them.

"Would you like to be my client? Would you like to be my client? How about you?" Eeek! It makes me cringe just picturing someone doing something like that. If **that's** your approach to client attraction, you're going to struggle! Worse than that, you're going to annoy everyone who comes near you. That's not the way you attract clients. That's a recipe for repelling them!

But, that's because of the underlying energy. You see, when you go out to "chase" a client like in the scenario above, you are sending out an energetic signature into the world that says, *"I am in need."* As we've already discussed, this is repulsive on an energetic level.

The most attractive person (to clients or spouses or any human being) is the one that doesn't need anything or anyone. That energetic signature is magnetic. The energetic signature of "need" repels.

It works the exact same way with money. The more you "need" it – and the stronger that signal is – the less money will want to be around you.

So, the same work you do to eradicate that feeling of need when it comes to attracting clients is going to serve you well when it comes to money. Hey, I didn't make up these rules, but I HAVE learned how to use them to my advantage. You can too!

How to Reset Your Relationship with Money

One of the quickest ways to "reset" your relationship with money is to put on a new pair of glasses, and take a fresh look at why your clients pay you.

We already spoke about this idea when it comes to why clients hire you. They aren't hiring you for your service; they are hiring you for what they get because of your service.

It's the same thing when it comes to paying you. Your clients aren't really paying for you to style their hair; they are paying you because they value what they get from the style **more** than they value their money!

Have you ever thought about just how valuable what you do actually is in the life of your client? Now you might say, *"Well, I'm just a hair stylist. I'm not saving lives or anything...."* While some people might describe that as being humble, I think there's more than that going on under the surface.

In fact, my guess is that more often than not, saying something like this betrays the true issue we're dealing with when it comes to money.

You Have Systematically Been Taught That You Are Small and Weak and Hardly Worthy of Much, Let Alone True Success

We won't mention any names, in order to protect the guilty, but understand that the system has no interest in you truly realizing how powerful you are. It has no need for a society full of people who truly understand how valuable they are. It has little desire to see a society that realizes it does not need to be "taken care of" – that it is perfectly capable of success on a very grand scale.

So, I'm going to tell it to you straight. I'm going to reveal the truth about you, your dreams, where you want to go, and what's been keeping you from getting there up until this point.

The truth is that you have been programmed to become your own worst enemy. You have been programmed to keep yourself small. That's what the system does. Do what you're told and you'll be okay. Stick out too much, and we'll bring you back in line. Actually, we'll train you to be so uncomfortable that you'll bring yourself back in line.

In any conversation, the person that is in control is the one who is asking the questions.

So listen up. This is work worth doing here. You can't feel worthless and be okay with accepting large amounts of money from your clients. That's like sending God a big GREEN LIGHT and a BIG RED LIGHT all at the same time! When you confuse God like that, what exactly is he supposed to send you?

Make Today the Day You Begin the Journey towards Sending out A Clear Signal about What You Want and How You Feel about Yourself

You are not here to play small, and your clients are not served by someone who thinks they aren't worth much.

Now, just a few moments ago, I mentioned how we stylists aren't really saving lives like a doctor or anything. But, aren't we? No, we're not saving lives in the physical world, but stick with me here as we think through this.

Imagine that client walking into your salon that **really** needs help. You can tell she is almost embarrassed about the way she looks. Her shoulders are drooping, her eyes immediately dart away when you make eye contact, her voice is weak, and she just doesn't sound confident.

She sits in your chair and you do your thing. As you work, you notice the expression on her face starts to change. You catch her stealing glances at herself in the mirror. You think you might have actually seen the beginnings of a smile.

Time passes…. You can feel the shift in her mood as you get close to the end.

When she walks out of your salon, for lack of a better way to describe it, she is a new person. Oh, you didn't really change the person she is. You helped restore her to the best version of herself.

The truth is, you **are** saving lives. It's just that you're doing it on an emotional level for your clients. And the work you do on that one life (your client) can ripple out through the rest of the world in amazing ways.

If you think that's a little bit over the top, my suggestion would be to UPGRADE your thinking about you. In fact, I challenge you to do it.

If you accept my challenge, and do it long enough, you are going to see some miraculous things.

And the reason why has everything to do with energy. You're going to see the world shifting before your eyes. It will seem like there's no reason for this, but the reason is actually quite simple.

When you can read my description above of that client whose life you "saved" and actually feel the feeling that comes with delivering that much value to someone, the signal you send out into the world will CHANGE.

How to Fill Your Being with the Energy That Is Attractive to EVERYTHING

So let's do a little exercise, shall we? This is really simple and really powerful.

First, take a deep breath and just let everything go that's swirling around in your mind. Don't worry. It'll all still be there when you come back.

Okay, so the first step is to recall a person from your past that really made you feel terrible about yourself – someone who was so cruel they made you feel like garbage. Just sit with that feeling for a moment and let it be.

Feels terrible doesn't it? Of course it does. I want you to get deep into that feeling because **this** is the feeling that most people carry around in themselves ALL THE TIME. Oh, it's not in their conscious thoughts all the time; it's deeper, much deeper. It's so deep you don't even realize it. The problem is that it controls just about every part of your life even if you aren't aware it's there.

Now let's go the other way....

Take another deep breath. Clear out all that junk we just waded through. Take another breath if you have to. Just breathe away that terrible feeling we conjured up.

When you are clear, let's move on....

The next picture to get in your mind is of sometime in your life where someone actually made you feel amazing about yourself. Maybe it was a parent or a loved one or a friend. Doesn't matter. It could even be your cat or dog! The important thing isn't how it looked. The important thing is how it felt.

That's a great feeling you are recalling, isn't it? It's warm and full, and it might have caused you just now to forget all of the "problems" you've been thinking about today.

That's the power of a feeling.

Now most people think the world happens TO them. Most people think that how you feel is simply a response to what's happening in your life.

Very few people realize that the reality is the exact opposite. What happens in your life is shaped by how you feel. That's because your feelings are just like a TV station that's broadcasting a signal 24/7.

What Is <u>Your</u> Station Broadcasting?

The first thing to become aware of in your dealings with prospects and clients is exactly what type of signal you are broadcasting. Are you walking around with that "worthless" feeling all the time? Or, are you walking around with that "valuable" feeling that you filled your being with just now?

Your answer to that question matters because the signal you are broadcasting is going out into the world and generating a response as it is received by others. There is no way you can become a successful stylist over the long term if you are sending out the signal of someone who is "worthless." Those two things are just incompatible, like oil and water.

If you can become a master at asking your prospects and clients the right questions, you will find that they pretty much sell themselves on working with you.

The first step is to become aware. The second step is to take control of your "broadcast."

The goal is to emit the type of energy that is attractive to everything you are looking for. It is the energy that is attractive to clients **and** to money.

Don't worry if all of this feels really weird at first. You're not going to erase decades of training about how valuable you are in just minutes. It's possible, I guess, but it sure didn't happen for me like that.

Nope…. This is a process, so don't be hard on yourself. Take one step at a time. Every day, practice generating this GREAT and VALUABLE feeling we've been talking about and carrying it through your day. You're going to be amazed at what begins to happen.

Okay… now that we've set the foundation, let's move on to getting paid!

Stop Charging Money for Haircuts

"What, Marquetta?!!? You just said we were going to talk about getting paid, and you're starting off by telling me NOT to charge for my services? Are you crazy?"

No, I'm not nuts. If you want to start charging premium fees for what you do, without working even harder than you already are, then the changes are going to actually begin on the inside and work out towards the world.

What I mean is that you want to do the work required INSIDE YOU to completely redefine what it is that you are charging for. Most stylists think that they are charging clients to stand behind the chair and style hair. On one level, that's true. But there's only so much you can charge for **that** before people start going somewhere else.

We've already established that a hairstyle isn't what the client is actually buying. We talked about the **real** results that come from the work you do in the lives of your clients. You want to rewire your brain so that you understand **that's** what your fee is for. It's far more valuable than just "cutting" or "coloring" hair. That's step 1. Changing your perception **alone** will lead to an immediate increase in your fees. And you'll get those fees provided you sell yourself on the idea of you actually believing you should be getting those fees. It's crazy how we are all self-fulfilling prophecies of our own making, but that seems to be how it works out. You don't get what you deserve. You get what you believe!

How Much Could One Piece of Paper be Worth?

Let me give you a quick example outside the hair industry to show you how valuable this is. Imagine you had a single sheet of white paper. Your goal was to walk out on the street and sell that piece of paper for as much money as possible.

How much do you think a person would pay for a single sheet of paper? A dollar? Ten cents? A penny? Well, maybe, if you're lucky. My hunch is that you'd have a hard time selling it, period, but who knows.

No one in their right mind is going to buy a single piece of paper for $100 or $1,000 or even $10,000. Right? Well, actually, it's half right and half wrong. Understanding why can have an enormous effect on your success in the hair industry.

I agree with you; no one is going to buy a single piece of paper alone for that kind of money. But imagine if there was something on that paper that completely changed the game? What if the paper simply was the carrier for a treasure that was valuable beyond measure? Then what could you sell that piece of paper for?

What if, scribbled on that sheet of paper, was a 100% proven, no catch, no fine print way to buy a **mansion** with only $1? Would knowledge like that make the piece of paper more valuable? You bet! In fact, that would change the game completely. Now, you could walk out onto the street and start asking for hundreds, thousands, even tens of thousands (or more!) of dollars… all for that single sheet of paper.

Technically, you'd be selling a sheet of paper. But that's not what the buyer would be buying. They'd be buying a secret potentially worth millions.

If you aren't already seeing the parallels between this example and your success in the hair industry, let me hammer it home.

Stop Charging for What You Do! Start Charging for What They Get Because of What You Do!

Just like earlier in the book where we talked about this idea in relation to your conversations with prospects and clients, this same idea extends into the world of money and fees.

If you are setting your fees based on your activity and not their result (what they get), then it's time to give yourself a raise. As you go here, I hope you're beginning to see that **you** are the one who holds the key to your own bright future. Life doesn't "happen to you." **You** happen to life! You are the reason that everything in your life is the way it is. This is good and bad, of course. But the bottom line is that if you want to change the type of fees you are changing, the only "permission" you have to ask is from the person staring back at you in the mirror!

Think back to that piece of paper we were just talking about. You're not going to like to spend the rest of your life selling "paper." No one pays a lot for just paper.

You want to be in the business of selling what that "paper" (the style, weave, color, or whatever you do for the client) **gets** your client. Those are two totally different things.

You make this change, first, in your head. You have to recalibrate your way of thinking. You have to stop thinking about what you do and start thinking about what they get.

Why Getting Money Seems So Hard

We've been trained in this world to think that attracting lots of money has to be hard. There's nothing easy, right? You have to endure some blood, sweat, and tears in order to get anywhere. If you don't invest a ton of effort, there's no way you can get much in return.

If you have thoughts like these running around wild inside your head, understand that **you** have been brainwashed.

Let me break it down for you so you never forget this…. This single idea that's coming up could change the course of your future and the future of your family.

Modern-day schooling was created to train people to work in factories. Up until that point in time, people did not sit in a room for eight or ten hours a day doing the same thing over and over again. That wasn't what life was like back then.

When the Industrial Revolution came along, the factories needed people to do just that. Factories needed a steady stream of employees willing and able to perform repetitive tasks all day long. They had to be able to sit still. They had to be able to follow orders. They had to be able to fit in.

Money is energy.

Is this beginning to sound like any place you know? This is exactly what **school** was designed to do. Yes, you learn some math and reading and other stuff along the way, but have you ever wondered why the focus in school is so much on getting the right answer? Have you wondered why **only the teacher's answer** is the right one? It's not because learning is the real goal.

School is designed to turn out employees who can **do the work**. Why do you think everyone makes fun of the "weird kid" at school? That's the system self-policing itself. You can't have an oddball in the factory. The system is designed to either get him in line or kick him out!

It wouldn't really work out if you started teaching those people that they could make thousands of dollars in just an hour. It wouldn't really work to show them that a single idea could completely transform their lives.

If too many people thought this, who'd want to work all day in the factory?! The most attractive person (to clients or spouses or any human being) is the one that doesn't need anything or anyone. That energetic signature is magnetic.

The most attractive person (to clients or spouses or any human being) is the one that doesn't need anything or anyone. That energetic signature is magnetic.

When you're trying to fill a factory, you need people who think they should be paid an "honest day's wages for an honest day's work." What's an honest day's work anyway? Who gets to define that? Why shouldn't your "work day" be two hours if you want it to be?

School is where we all were taught that attracting money is difficult. If we don't put in a ton of effort, how in the world should we expect to get much back? This is factory worker thinking, and you have no place doing it. This is the type of thinking that leads to stylists standing behind the chair 24/7 and barely being able to make ends meet!

You have been fooled, and TODAY is the day you can decide to wake up.

Dealing with the Turbulence

Now, changing programming that is so deeply ingrained in us is no small feat! Don't worry if you experience some "turbulence" along the way. You've been allowing your life to run on someone else's "programs" for a long time, so you've had a ton of practice. And starting a **new** habit can be a little bit bumpy.

In fact, I can just hear what some stylists who read this chapter are going to say.

"Marquetta, I can't just start charging more for what I do.... Even if I start focusing on charging for 'what they get,' why would my clients pay more just to come to me? If I charge too much, they will just go someplace else!"

This is pure factory thinking and I'll show you why. First of all, factory thinking is about modularization. If employee number 874 calls in sick on Tuesday, there are 400 other people who could happily do the job. It doesn't take a lot to sit by the machine, and press the red button 4,000 times per day.

The entire world of the factory is about the assembly line. It was about extracting all of the specific tasks required to make something and then training people in those tasks. This would make the people easily replaceable. When one of them decided to be "human" for a day, there was someone else who could step in.

<u>YOU</u> <u>ARE</u> <u>NOT</u> <u>A</u> <u>FACTORY</u> <u>WORKER</u>. And if you are going to make sure the world is clear about that, then you have to get clear about it first. You need to get out of that mindset and install a new one. The new one has little to no connection between EFFORT and RETURN. In other words, it's entirely possible to put in a little bit of effort and get

a lot back. I'm not saying you won't work, but it's going to be a different type of work.

When that fear pops up of your clients going to someone else, you need to upgrade your own view of yourself. You are **not** replaceable. The work that another stylist does with a client is not the same work they would get from you.

How I Became a One-of-a-Kind Stylist and How You Can Too!

A lot of what we cover in this book is focused on making you a "one-of-a-kind" stylist in the hair industry. The fact is, you already are. But you have to approach things a little differently than the average stylist in order to make sure your prospects and clients understand this.

The reason why is that if your clients can only get what you do from you, that tilts things in your favor in a big way.

Here's the thing: you don't have to be the best stylist in the world to succeed. You have to be good. Sure, you can be great. Be as great as you can be. Fulfill on the potential you know you have. The truth is, no matter how great a stylist you become, there will **always** be someone "better." This isn't meant to make you feel bad. Actually, if you truly "get this," it's one of the best things I could possibly tell you.

Most stylists think that in order to attract clients on demand, they have to be the best. Not true! In fact, your skill as a stylist is probably 60% of it. So, yes, be good at what you do. But that's not enough!

Your clients are going to search you out not just because of how you style hair, but because of WHO YOU ARE and what that means to them.

How do you get that to happen? The Platform. That's your signal to the world. Now that we've gotten the signal clear and are ready to receive abundance, it's time to amplify everything. There are a couple of steps to this, but I'll walk you through it. If your mind hasn't been "reset" during the previous chapters, the next few are going to take care of it. So, let's go!

....

The truth is that you have been programmed to become your own worst enemy.

....

8

PACKING YOURSELF
UP IN A BOX

One of the rarest things in the life of a stylist is LEVERAGE. Leverage is the term I use to describe getting more out of something than you put in. I don't mean it in a lazy way, though. Leverage is all about creating 10X of something that only required 1X of ingredients.

In other words, you invest a certain amount of effort, but the payoff is huge.

This is the exact opposite situation that most stylists experience every day of their lives. Stylists generally have zero leverage in their business. They do work. They get paid. They style hair. They get paid. They do a weave. They get paid. It's a 1-1 relationship. Effort in, result out.

Now, this beats sitting in an office cubicle somewhere, but still, we can improve on it in a major way. We need a "lever." We need something that you can use to do the work ONCE and then reap the benefit over and over and over again.

Imagine if you could "clone" yourself and then have all of the copies of you working all day long. Now, that would be leverage. It would probably be a little weird to see so many of "you" running around, but it would definitely lighten the load. Just think, you could work with many different clients all at the same time. That'd be a good day!

Now, of course, I'm joking about the cloning. It's not going to happen, but we're going to do the next best thing. We're going to "package" you up in a way that you can actually be helping a lot of people all at once without working any harder.

The Power of Product

What I'm talking about is "product" – not product like we're used to using in the salon. I'm talking about other products – products you have created. Products that take some of your expertise, package it up, and send it all over the world to people who can benefit from it.

As stylists, it's pretty easy to forget just how much we know about a lot of things. From color to cutting to hair care, make-up, going natural, and more, there's a LONG list of things we know. In fact, you've probably forgotten more things about hair than most people will ever know!

But all that knowledge, expertise, and experience can't do anyone any good if it's stuck there in your head. It can do your clients good – one at a time. We're talking about **leverage** here, remember? So "one at a time" doesn't qualify as leverage, not the kind I'm talking about.

I've spent more than a decade helping women all over the world in this very way. It started years ago when my husband asked me if I wanted to start selling things on the Internet. At the time, I didn't know anything about it. I was already taking clients back then, but the idea of making a DVD or something ONCE and then selling it over and over and over again was pretty darn exciting!

So, we got started. From one product we built an entire world of products and services. All of them have one thing in common. They are all different ways I've taken what I know and what I can do and (sometimes **literally**) put them "in a box" to be sold all over the world!

But I'm a Stylist! I Do Hair! I Can't Make Products!

I'm not in the business of excuses. I don't do it for myself and because I care about your future, I'm not going to accept them from you.

If your mind's first response to all of this "product making" talk is to come up with excuses for why you can't do it, let's just deal with those issues right away. All of the knowledge you have and the experience you have and the insight you have can't help the world until you get it out into a form that people can use! Tell that little voice in your head that's saying *"I can't do this"* to go take a hike, and let's get to work!

The Good News

The good news is that by walking through the process a little while ago where we were building your Platform, you've already done a lot of the thinking required to get the strategy right for your products.

Products are packaged up solutions to problems. Earlier in this journey, we talked about all of the "pain" that your prospective clients experience that you are able to solve. That's the "pain" you relieve with your products. But, when you do it with a product, **you** aren't the one who is actually doing the work!

Rather than talk through this in a theoretical way, I'm going to take you through the creation of one of MY product lines to show you how you can do it.

This product turned into something BIG over the years, but you don't have to start that way. Products can be small. They can be very specific, and they can be focused on solving one very small (but important) problem for your clients.

The Reason I Learned How to Make Lace Wigs

I started my first website online selling DVDs about how to braid hair. From cornrows to kinky twists to micro braids and weaves, I made products about <u>all</u> of them. And it was exciting!

I'd plan out the DVD, and then my husband would film me walking through the "here's how you do it" steps. These products fed my family for many years!

However, for this example, I want to show you how to come up with product ideas by thinking of "problems" that you can solve for your clients and then package.

As my business grew over the years, I started getting emails – a lot of emails – from customers asking if I could help them deal with loved ones who had lost their hair as a result of treatment for cancer.

It's crazy how we are all self-fulfilling prophecies of our own making, but that seems to be how it works out. You don't get what you deserve. You get what you believe!

One day it all hit home when my mother was diagnosed with breast cancer and lost all of her hair as a result of her chemotherapy. To be frank, I was probably more affected by this than she was, and I became determined to do something about it.

I wanted to help my mom feel like herself again by restoring her hair and giving her something to smile about when she looked in the mirror.

So I dug DEEP into the world of lace wigs and figured out how to use them to make my mom look great!

Once I perfected the approach for myself, I turned what I had learned into a product that could help other women all over the world. The Lace Wig Training System took six months to build and took me over 200 hours to get on film! It was a lot of work, but I packed everything into it that I knew about making lace wigs. Back then, putting all of this together was no small feat. However, these days, with the tools that we all have access to, doing something like this is far less complicated.

What I ended up with was a product that finally made it possible, for any woman who wanted to do the work, to make a beautiful lace wig.

Multimedia, Multiple Levels of Value

The thing you want to keep in mind is that a single problem you are able to solve for your clients can turn into several (or more!) products.

You can solve the same problem (i.e. how to make lace wigs) at different levels, at different prices, in different media.

With the Lace Wig Training System, it began as a product I could ship anywhere in the world. It has DVDs, booklets, worksheets, and more – everything someone needs to learn how to make lace wigs all on their own. But then it grew because people who got the System wanted more. They wanted hands-on instruction to help them to get better more quickly.

That's how another product – the Lace Wig Mastery Training Seminar – was born. Granted, I can't put this one "in a box" and ship it out. Instead, I set up things so everyone comes to me! This is the very same knowledge and experience but delivered in a completely new way for people who want to be side-by-side as they learn to make lace wigs.

I tell you all of this for those of you who are thinking, *"Well, I really only know how to do one thing well...."* I'm here to say, **that's enough!**

Just think about what you know and what you love to do. Ask yourself about the problems you can solve for clients. Ask yourself how you could package up that solution (or even part of it) to make the lives of your clients better?

At first you may not come up with too many ideas. That's fine. There's no way most couch potatoes could hop up and run a marathon the first time either. Your mind is just like a muscle. The more you work it out in certain ways, the stronger it will become. So don't worry if the going is a little rocky at the beginning. It'll get easier!

But if I Solve These Problems for My Clients, Why Would They Come to See Me?

If that little voice in your head is telling you that if you help your clients via products no one is going to come and see you, read this next sentence slowly.

The way to succeed isn't to make sure you "get your piece of the pie." The way to succeed in abundance is to figure out how to make the pie bigger!

A lot of the reason so many stylists struggle is because they approach the world and their business as if there isn't enough to go around. When you have that feeling in your gut, your reality will show you exactly what your signal is asking for. That's how it works. Your reality molds itself around the signals that you are sending out into the world. If you are FEELING lack, that's exactly what you will see.

So please make a commitment to yourself that YOU are not going to go through life this way. Let the other stylists do that. You will give and serve freely, giving it everything you've got. You will do that because you have the confidence that it will come back to you many times over!

How to Put Your Products to Work for You, Even If You **Never** Sell One!

Developing your ability to "package up" your expertise in product form has another benefit, too, apart from all of the income that you can generate doing it.

In fact, I'd recommend you create your own products, even if you choose to give them all away!

Writing a book is just one example where this makes perfect sense. A lot of authors write books and then try to sell them. If you've ever tried to sell a book, it's not that easy!

First of all, you can't really sell a book for more than $20 or so. So if you were actually going to use book sales to support you and your family, you'd have to sell A LOT of them! It's not something I'd recommend.

But let's say you write a book about your approach to hair and beauty, and give them to people that ask about your services. Yes, you'll pay a few bucks to get each copy printed, but think of it as an investment in your client attraction system. That money **will** come back… and it will most likely bring friends!

It basically becomes your business card – a "product" that you created that will do more to **sell you** more than anything you could ever say to a prospective client. I can tell you from experience that it's WAY more valuable than any business card I've ever had.

School is designed to turn out employees who can do the work.

Let's say you are a prospective client looking for a high-end weave. Who are **you** going to call? Are you going to go to the stylist who can't stop blabbing about herself, or are you going to go to the stylist who "wrote the book about weaves?" Easy answer.

So, when you are looking to attract clients, products can be a way to generate additional streams of income, or they can be used to attract high-paying clients. They can also be used for both things at the same time! Can you imagine your future clients actually sending you money for products that prove to them that they should hire you? It's a beautiful position to be in, and it is something **you** can do.

There is really no limit to how creative you can get when you commit yourself to helping people.

You can make audio products, video products, written products, seminars or workshops, or other stuff I've never even thought of! Really, this is a skill to develop. I refer to it as "the ability to help your clients" even if they never hire you! Everybody wins. Over time, the development of your products takes the pressure off you having to get clients to make ends meet.

The funny part about this is that the less you need clients, the more easily they tend to show up!

Okay, so let's keep going. Next up, I'm going to reveal to you THE secret that powers all of this. It's something that I think is probably responsible for more normal people building extraordinary lives and businesses than anything else I can think of!

To use this secret, you don't have to be rich or famous or even popular. It can transform your life, even if you are starting with nothing. It's certainly transformed my life. And I DID start with nothing....

9

MY MILLION DOLLAR SECRET

So, I have a little secret… It's a secret about how I created my own success in the hair industry **without** standing behind a chair 12 hours a day.

I've used this one secret to generate millions of dollars in income over the years. Now, I tell you that number not to brag – I hate people who brag – but to, instead, make it clear that this is something that works. Goodness knows, I don't do this just for the money. Money is great, and it helps me to provide for my family. But do you know what is better?

What is better is having someone look you in the eye and tell you how your work has changed his or her life. You know another thing that's "better" than money? When a woman comes up to you at a seminar and talks about how her lace wig made her feel beautiful again. Money can't buy those things. Money is just a byproduct of adding value to the lives of other people.

But understand that if you want to add an enormous amount of value to those in your circles, certain approaches are more effective than others. The approach I'm about to reveal is one of the most effective ways I know!

A New Way of Thinking About Anything Related to Business

What I'm talking about is a new way to think about you, your business, and how you get the word out about your products and services.

To illustrate what I mean, let's take the "average" stylist and talk through her approach to advertising her services.

I can see it now. She decides to advertise her services in a local magazine. She has an entire page that she can use and can say pretty much whatever she wants. The stylist wants to communicate that she offers high-end services for very discriminating clients.

She ends up with something she thinks is stunning. Covering most of the page is a picture of a very beautiful woman. Underneath the picture is the name of her salon and the phone number. That's it. A very simple, understated advertisement.

Unfortunately, something like this has a very small chance of actually working.

The reason why it won't work leads right into this "secret" I've been talking about. It basically comes down to using a specific strategy for just about everything you offer to the world.

It's called "direct response."

Here's the Opposite of What We're Going to Do

You know those big billboards you see when you're driving down the highway? Those are advertising, right? Right. So think of a billboard you've seen, maybe one for a car or something. The content of the billboard is usually pretty similar. There's usually a big picture of the car, maybe the name of the car, and then a tagline or slogan or something.

Leverage is all about creating 10X of something that only required 1X of ingredients.

Those billboards are NOT CHEAP. But here's a question that's going to get right to the heart of my "million dollar secret." The question is this one: **How do you know if that billboard actually works? How do you know if it actually sells cars?**

The answer is that there's no way you can know. There is no way to know if that billboard leads to ZERO car sales or 100 or 1,000. So how does the person who is actually paying for that billboard know if they should **keep** paying for it? Again, they don't. They just keep it going because that's how the car business works.

It's the very same thing with the advertisement I just talked about at the beginning of this chapter – the one where the stylist just put a beautiful woman on the page with the phone number of the salon. How could a stylist know if that advertisement worked or not? How could she know whether that investment is something that's worth making again? She can't.

This approach to marketing and advertising is what people in the industry call "image advertising." They call it that because it basically publicizes your brand in a very generic way. This type of advertising is what people do when they "want to get the word out." That's a pretty generic goal, if I must say so. If that's your goal – to "get the word out" – what's the sign you're looking for to prove you achieved it?

"Million Dollar Secret Rule" #1:
If the Marketing or Advertising Costs Money and You Can't Prove It Worked, Do Something Else!

As busy stylists, we're working with limited time and limited resources. We don't have the budgets of big car companies, and frankly, we're a whole lot smarter than they are. Think about it. Car companies hire ad agencies. Ad agencies don't want to get fired, so ad agencies have no interest in the car companies figuring out whether the ad worked or not. The more "in the dark" their clients remain, the bigger the chances they'll keep them as clients!

It's really backwards if you think about it, and it's not an approach that we can afford to take. We have to be smart. We have to make our investments go **much** further. And most of all, we can't be flying blind when we're spending money on marketing and advertising.

But this isn't ONLY something to keep in mind when you are spending money. It even applies when you are investing your TIME. You want to pursue client attraction activities that you can measure. If you can measure it, you can improve it.

So, let's get specific about what I'm talking about. I told you that this different approach to marketing was called "direct response." The reason it's called this is simple: it is set up to generate some sort of DIRECT RESPONSE from your target audience.

You are asking for something *very* specific. That way, it becomes very clear whether or not you actually got what you asked for!

This might be hard to wrap your head around at first, so let me give you an example. This is an example of what you might call a "direct response email" that I sent to my list of subscribers on my birthday one year. Read through it, and then we'll go back and take it apart to see how it works.

****

SUBJECT LINE: *It's My Birthday Today, But I'm Hooking YOU Up! (Huge Coupon Inside)*

Hey it's Marquetta, I hope your Thursday is off to a great start!

Well, today I turn 32 years old and have to say, I'm thankful to God for allowing me to see another year.

I'm also thankful for my family, husband, kids, and of course YOU!

There isn't a day that goes by that I'm not thankful

for you and the trust you've put in me to deliver the information you want on hair and beauty. I take that trust very seriously and I want to say thank you.

So, what I'm going to is give you 32% OFF anything you want at two of my websites which are BraidsByBreslin.com and LaceWigTrainingCenter.com.

All you have to do is enter "32" when checking out and 32% will be taken off your order right then and there.

This coupon will expire on April 17th.

We've been in business around 9 years and I can count on one hand the times I've sent a coupon code out, I just never do it, it's not part of the way we do business.

But if you've ever wanted to grab a product at a huge discount, this is the time for sure.

To visit the websites, go to:

http://www.braidsbybreslin.com

or...

http://www.lacewigtrainingcenter.com

Then simply add whatever you want to the cart and enter "32" for your 32% off discount.

I hope you enjoy and I'm personally going to take the rest of the day off for a much needed break!

Talk soon,

Marquetta Breslin

P.S. I'm not blogging about this and nobody else will know about this huge discount. This is between me and my faithful customers and subscribers so please keep this discount between us, thanks!

The coupon for 32% off will expire on April 17th.

****

This is the approach to marketing and advertising I'm suggesting you learn. Make it a habit to think this way. It will supercharge your client attraction efforts and keep you from wasting time and money on things that don't work.

So, let's go through this email so you can learn about the building blocks to marketing done the SMART way.

Now, when you send out an email like this, **the subject line** pretty much makes or breaks your results. If your subject line is bad, no one is going to open the email – which means it's almost like you didn't even send it! You want to put yourself in the shoes of your reader and ask, *"What subject line would get ME to open this email?"*

An email has a subject line, but letters, brochures, postcards, and magazine ads do not. The equivalent thing there is the HEADLINE. The headline (or subject line) does two things. First, it calls out your audience and broadcasts who this is for. Second, it gives a clear benefit to the reader for WHY they should read whatever the piece is.

In my example, the subject line is pretty compelling. People know they are about to be presented with a great opportunity to save money.

Next up is what I call "the offer." This is how you talk about what it is you are advertising – what is it that you are offering to the readers of your marketing or advertising. You want this to be **specific.** Notice I'm not saying, *"Hey call me!"* That's not specific. No, I'm super specific here. I am offering my readers the opportunity to save 32% OFF of my products. That's very, very specific.

Next, the offer is measurable. That means I can see if it worked or NOT. How is it measurable? It's measurable because I've included a "coupon code" to be used when my subscriber orders. All I have to do is count up the number of orders that come in with the coupon code, and I KNOW (we're not guessing here!) just how effective this was.

It always makes me a little sad when I see a stylist advertising with absolutely no way to measure if that ad is working or not. A lot of stylists probably think that advertising and marketing just don't work. This is one of the biggest reasons why they think that! But after reading this, you will never be one of those people.

Okay, next up, the DEADLINE.

....

Deadlines are motivating, so that's why we include them in just about every piece of marketing and advertising we do. They work. Don't forget it!

....

Think about your clients and how you sell your services. There's really not a reason they should call you **today** vs. waiting two weeks right? Sure, their hair might look worse over those two weeks, but still, people are busy. Your client might have intended to call you to schedule an appointment, but then the cat knocked over the coffee on the computer, and the child threw a bunch of crayons in the toilet. Before you know it, that call your client was going to make to you gets lost in the shuffle of life.

That's where the DEADLINE comes in. It gives the reader of your marketing or advertising a real and believable reason to act sooner than later. You'll see in my email. I had a firm deadline. Use the coupon code **before** the deadline, and you put 32% of your money right back in your pocket. Use the coupon code **after** the deadline, and you have to pay full price. Deadlines are motivating, so that's why we include them in just about every piece of marketing and advertising we do. They work. Don't forget it!

So, just to recap, when you are putting marketing and advertising together to feed your client attraction systems, these are the components you want to include:

1. You use some sort of method for "calling out your audience" and giving them a reason to read what you have. On a postcard or flyer, this is a HEADLINE. On an email, it is a SUBJECT line.

2. You are making a specific offer. It could be something like get 20% off, or "I'm making five 'Over-the-Top Beauty Packages' available" or something else. Get creative! Just be **specific**.

3. The response to your offer needs to be easily measurable. How many people take you up on your offer? You can use coupon codes, or you could use different phone numbers or email addresses – something so that you know whether your marketing/advertising is working or not.

4. There is a reason to act now not later. Make this REAL. You do not want to be "hypey" or fake or lie to people. Those acts are forbidden – not only because lying is WRONG, but also because you will damage the trust you have built with your future clients. Do not do it. Be real, be authentic, and be confident. You can use deadlines, or you can use limited quantity numbers. Again, you can be creative here.

This is Not Only a More Effective Way of Marketing! It's a Completely Different Way of Thinking!

Earlier in the book, I gave you an example of my "Advanced Hair Analysis" letter I sent out to prospective clients in the area of my salon. If you go back and read through that letter, you'll see all of these "direct response" things in that letter.

There was a specific offer, a tracking mechanism, and a reason to act sooner than later. I didn't include a headline in the excerpt I printed, but there **was** one on the letter I sent. It was **A Special Invitation for Summerville Women Who Won't Settle For Anything Less Than Looking Beautiful**.

Can you see how this approach to things is about 100% the opposite of what most stylists are out there doing? They have no idea this whole world exists. I'm all for helping people, but since **you** are reading this book and they aren't, we'll just keep all this "our little secret."

Not only is this a more effective and less risky way to go, but it's also going to keep you from wasting your money on things that don't work. Sure, you'll have to learn through trial and error a little bit about what does work and what does not, but at least you won't be guessing like most people do.

The longer you go and the more you do things this way, the smarter you will get about what actually works to attract the clients you want to work with. You will generate bigger results, more easily, with less effort.

Okay, it's time to wrap this up. I have one more ingredient for you that's going to help in your client attraction efforts. So let's dig in....

10

The Missing Ingredients

Whew! We have covered a lot of ground in a really short time. If your head hurts, you're not alone! But don't worry, I packed this book with as much real-world info as I could so you could use this, as a resource, for years to come.

The fact is, most stylists are struggling unnecessarily when it comes to client attraction. They have no idea what type of signal they are sending out into the world, let alone how to change it.

The fact is, most stylists are struggling unnecessarily when it comes to client attraction.

The result, of course, is they end up attracting clients they really shouldn't be working with. Those are the clients that want cheap; those are the clients that complain about your work; and those are the clients that never come back!

If you've learned nothing else from our journey together so far, never forget that **you** are the reason the clients you have are showing up.

You are basically like a beacon sending a certain type of signal out into the world. Depending on the flavor of that signal, it's noticed by different people.

That's a pretty tough pill to swallow if you're in a situation where you're not getting the right clients. In fact, if you can take full responsibility for everything that's happening in your life and business, you will be in a very small, elite, and powerful crowd.

With Responsibility Comes an Enormous Amount of Power

Before we wrap this up, there are a couple of things I want to cover with you. You could probably call this chapter, the "tough love" chapter. Know that I tell you all of this because I really do care deeply about your future. I have been blessed with my path in life, and I am on a MISSION to share what I know with as many stylists who are ready to listen.

If you've made it this far, you qualify for some of the most important parts of my message.

You'll notice that at the beginning of this book about client attraction, we actually started by talking about what was going on between your ears. We talked about you, your thoughts, feelings, and beliefs about yourself. From there, we widened out and connected you with your world of clients.

We did things in this order for a reason. You create your life; it is not handed to you to live out.

The raw materials that become various parts of your life are the SIGNALS you send out from your own being into the world. Those signals (energy!) interact with other things in the world and then bounce back to you.

....

You create your life; it is not handed to you to live out.

....

Your thoughts are signals, your words are signals, and your actions are signals. These are the raw materials that have become your life! So the first thing to realize is that everything that is in your life and business is there because you put it there! All of those things are supposed to be there, whether you like them or not!

I'm sure you don't have to think too hard to come up with someone you know that's a "complainer." We all have someone in our circles that just can't stop complaining about everything. Nothing is ever right for them!

Have you ever thought about a "complaint" in terms of energy? It's simply raw material that you send out into the world. But a complaint is raw material with a particular flavor. It goes out and resonates with other similar energy and then comes back with friends. What that means is that sending out "complaint-flavored" energy brings back to you more reasons to complain! Never forget that **like attracts like**.

The 7-Day Challenge

If you're serious about this client attraction stuff and about completely transforming your life (yes, I think BIG), then here's a little exercise I'm challenging you to do.

For the next 7 days, get in the habit of monitoring ALL of your outgoing "signals." This is hard work so go in with your eyes open!

What I mean is to begin to develop your awareness of the signals you are sending out at the level of feeling, thought, word, and deed.

Most people are totally oblivious to this. They just go through their lives like they are in a trance. They are NOT AWARE. This is what I want to help you change. I want to help "wake you up" in a way you've never been woken up before. Just a warning – once you wake up, there's no going back in the box!

My hunch is that what you're going to find over the next 7 days is that you are sending out a lot more low quality signals than you probably thought! Before you can change them, you have to know they are there.

This skill is important because it affects the people you attract to you in a major way.

The point here isn't to shut down your feelings or your normal human reactions. We don't want to go through life like a robot! So when someone does something that makes you mad, go ahead and be mad. The trick is to **realize you are mad** and to begin to understand that being mad and continuing to be mad is a conscious choice you are making. It is a choice with consequences. You are free to choose either way, but the choice you make requires that you be prepared for the consequences. That is the powerful way to go through your life and business.

....

I know for a fact that it is 100% IMPOSSIBLE to fill your being with gratitude for everything you have AND also have any leftover space to put in a feeling of neediness.

....

Over time, you will develop the ability to "control" your signals. And as an extension, you will figure out how to exert enormous control over your life.

The clock is ticking. Life is short. Fill it with you becoming the best version of yourself. That's what all of this is about. And that leads us into my second "tough love" message.

No One Will Respect Your Time until <u>YOU</u> Do

A lot of stylists talk about how they want respect. But their actions communicate something to the world that will ensure that respect never, EVER comes.

No one will respect you until YOU respect you. It goes back to the thing about "signals." How you think about yourself… those thoughts are ANOTHER signal!

If you want to stand out above the average stylist, start doing things the average stylist won't do. One of those things is to emit the signal that you have respect for yourself. This isn't just thinking here. I'm talking about it carrying through to your actions.

I've seen salons where the stylist comes in 30 minutes late for an appointment with a client. Then, while she's shampooing her client, she's yapping on the phone about something that just doesn't matter to anyone but her. Now, if that's the stylist's first appointment of the day, every other one of her clients is going to suffer. Personally, I've experienced stuff that's even worse! Once I was getting my hair done, and the stylist set me under the dryer. She said she had forgotten her flat iron and needed to run across the street to get one.

She came back – 90 minutes later – with bags full of clothes! She'd gone shopping!

Now you might know someone like this. You might even be like this stylist! Remember, we're taking full responsibility here for everything in our lives… and that includes our own behavior!

You might hear about a "late" stylist or even mine who went shopping and think, *"Boy, she's not going to have many clients if she keeps this up."* In other words, you might think this is going to be the cause of bad stuff coming down the future (like losing all your clients).

But I don't see it quite that way. This type of behavior isn't the cause; it's the effect of something else. It's the result of something inside that stylist. Something inside her is causing this type of behavior. That something, for lack of a better way to put it, is simply that she doesn't respect herself.

You can't respect someone else if you can't respect yourself. Being late, rude, inconsiderate, or totally oblivious just betrays what you think about YOU. Again, we're dealing with truth here. And only you know if this applies to you.

If it does, change it. If it doesn't apply to you, just move on. When you respect YOURSELF enough to be where you say you're going to be at the time you say you are going to be there, it communicates that you respect yourself enough to treat yourself WELL. This signal is going to attract clients who will treat you the very same way.

This is why I look at so many stylists and just wish they realized the type of leader they could truly be. They are so caught up in trying to make ends meet that they forget they could be playing on an entirely different level.

Okay, I've got another one – another piece of "tough love" that's actually so powerful, it's about as close to real magic as I've ever seen.

How to Eradicate Need in 3 Seconds

We talked earlier in this book about how "not needing" clients is actually the best way to attract them. Going back to the animal kingdom, if you chase something, it runs away. It's the same with clients. So the more you "need" them and the more they feel that, the less likely they are going to want to take a step towards you.

Again, we're dealing with signals you send out in the form of energy. Are you beginning to see how this single topic pretty much affects every area of your business and life?

So what's my "magical" solution to help you eradicate need? Even if you have bills to pay? Even if the rent is late? Even if you're not sure (yet) where the next client is coming from?

No, I'm not going to give you a bunch of positive affirmations to say or any abundant thoughts to meditate on. While those work for some people, there's something far more powerful you can use that can instantly eradicate need from your being. When that is gone, you can send out the right signals again that bring the clients.

What I'm talking about is a very powerful 9-letter word:

GRATITUDE

I know for a **fact** that it is 100% IMPOSSIBLE to fill your being with gratitude for everything you have AND also have any leftover space to put in a feeling of neediness. It's almost like the more gratitude you feel, the farther away that "needy" feeling gets.

Gratitude and need are kind of like oil and water. They don't mix, they won't mix, and they can't mix. So, if you put ONE of those things into your body on purpose, the other one has to get out of town!

....

I know for a fact that it is 100% IMPOSSIBLE to fill your being with gratitude for everything you have AND also have any leftover space to put in a feeling of neediness.

....

Try it just for ONE day. You'll see it's not as easy as you would think. That's because we've all been trained to pretty much spend our days thinking about all of the things we **don't** have. This sets up a terrible downward spiral. We focus on what we don't have, and that attracts more "not having." And so it continues. It continues until you break the cycle. You break the cycle with gratitude.

Just think about all of the things in your life that you have to be thankful for. Really focus on filling your entire being with that "being thankful" feeling. Keep that feeling going. Keep it going for a minute, then 10 minutes, then an hour, then all day long.

I'm not highlighting all of this just to make you feel good. This is a strategy that brings enormous benefits to you on multiple levels. Yes, you will actually **feel** better, but you'll also become way more attractive to others, including prospective clients.

The next time a new prospect calls you on the phone, instead of trying to "close the deal," how about you start off with saying a short prayer of gratitude for the opportunity to help someone. That's an entirely different feeling to have when you enter a sales situation. You fill yourself with gratitude and the person on the other end will feel it. I guarantee you that they will feel it.

Okay, we've got just ONE more, but you've got to read this last one. Why? Because it's going to "save the day" more than once in this business. Like all of these other items I'm wrapping up our little journey with, this is yet one more dose of "tough love." The medicine might not taste good going down, but it does amazing things if you let it work.

How to Stand in Your Power Even When Everything Goes to $*#@!

You don't have to be in this business very long before you are going to end up having a BAD day. Maybe a client yells at you. Maybe three clients don't even show. Maybe you find out that some other stylist in town has been spreading lies about you. Maybe, one of your longest-standing clients looks at you after you get done with her hair and says, *"I hate it!"* And then she starts bawling right there in the salon.

These things happen, and they are not fun. I'm going to share with you a secret I learned about how not to fall apart. In fact, this secret will completely flip your thinking around about what all of these "bad" things mean.

First of all, I want to remind you of the commitment we made a few pages back. EVERYTHING in our life is our responsibility. That includes the good, the bad, and the ugly.

The first thing I'd recommend you do when things go south is to look at the situation and say, *"I OWN THIS."* Take responsibility for it. Don't put the blame on someone else. Don't try to deflect it from yourself. Just stand there, own up to it, and say, "This is my situation."

Now, we were trained in school that "confession" is a terrible thing. It certainly feels terrible, doesn't it? Well, like so many other things, the truth is actually the exact opposite. When you go through life taking responsibility for everything that comes your way, you will emit a power that is extremely attractive.

When you stand up and say, *"This is my mess,"* you can actually feel the pressure release. It actually takes a weight off your shoulders. If you've never done this, you might not believe me, but you have to try it.

The first step is personal responsibility. The second step is to actually look at the mess and ask yourself, *"What is the message in this that I am meant to see?"* You see, I don't think there are accidents in life. Everything happens for a reason. Let me rephrase that. I think everything happens for a lesson. If you GET the lesson, you stop having to REPEAT the lesson. It's totally up to you which direction you choose.

"What is my lesson here?" Start getting in the habit of asking yourself that, and you'll see an amazing shift in your reality. You may not realize how rare of a quality this is. But if you install this as a habit for you, you

will experience amazing transformation on just about every level. Your clients will feel it. They will feel that you are the "real deal."

....

EVERYTHING in our life is our responsibility.

....

11

LOOKING FORWARD

Now we've come to the end of this journey together, in one way, this is the end. But it's really just the beginning. It's the beginning of you putting what we've covered into action.

I want to leave you with a few important thoughts that are going to help you use what you've learned to build a client attraction system most stylist's probably wouldn't even believe!

Just a word of warning…

Our society is addicted to speed. Everyone wants everything fast, cheap, and easy. You probably know by now that very little good comes fast, cheap, or easy. Everything has its price. Everything good takes time.

The most important idea I can leave you with is that client attraction done right is <u>not</u> a one-time event; it is a never-ending process. You might hear that and think that's a bad thing. It's not. In fact, the fact that it **is** a never-ending process is one of the greatest opportunities you have.

Other stylists will be out there doing everything they can to "get clients." You will be investing your time, focus, and energy in building the SYSTEM that gets you the clients.

The first approach might get you some clients, but the second approach builds you an ASSET that will pay you in "clients" over and over and over again.

So here's how I recommend you think about this:

You Are Pushing a Snowball up the Hill

That basically sums it up right there. At first, your client attraction efforts might be small and slow. That's fine. That's how you begin. I'd recommend that you enjoy the process. Don't just focus on "When am I going to be done with this?" That's going to lead to misery.

Over time, your "snowball" is going to get bigger. It might be hard to get it to the top of the hill. But once it starts to roll down the other side of the hill, watch out! I'd tell you it is magic because that's exactly what it looks like and that's how it feels. But it's not magic. It's just strategy coupled with consistent action.

Now that you've come to this point of our journey, you know what you need to know to make it all a reality for you.

While you might not be able to conceive of it now, you might want to start asking yourself, *"What do I do when I start getting too many clients?"* That's a good problem to have, of course. Given what we've covered about product creation and other ways to help a large number of people, you shouldn't have any problem coming up with ideas.

For now, understand that you know what few stylists will ever know about how to attract clients on demand.

I'm excited for you! It's going to be an amazing ride!

ABOUT THE AUTHOR

Marquetta Breslin is the co-founder of Breslin Products, LLC. She is a licensed cosmetologist, educator, and author of *The Black Hair Answer Book* and *Chained To The Chair No More*. She has educated some of the industry's top professionals, including Oscar-nominated makeup artists and *Vogue Magazine* Editorial Stylists. Marquetta has been featured in Sophisticate's *Black Hair Magazine*, BNB, Business 2.0, CNNMoney.com, NBC, and ABC. Her custom lace wigs have graced cancer patients and Hollywood feature films. She is the creator of systems such as "Lace Wig Training System," "Cutting Mastery," and "Million Dollar Stylist®," which have reached more than 50,000 customers in over 55 countries. She is also a professional speaker and trainer, mainly at live events, such as her Lace Wig Mastery Training Seminar and Million Dollar Stylist® LIVE! For booking information, please visit MarquettaBreslin.com.